STEVE BACKSHALL'S WILDLIFE ADVENTURER'S GUIDE

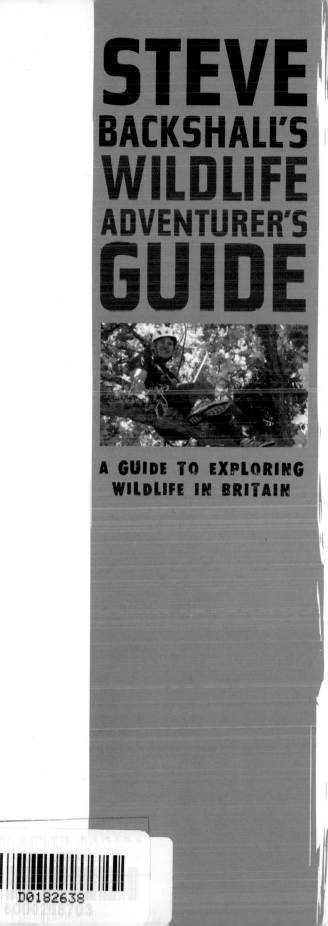

A GUIDE TO EXPLORING WILDLIFE IN BRITAIN

STEVE BACKSHALL'S WILDLIFE ADVENTURER'S GUIDE

A GUIDE TO EXPLORING WILDLIFE IN BRITAIN

BLOOMSBURY
LONDON · OXFORD · NEW YORK · NEW DELHI · SYDNEY

First published in 2009 by New Holland Publishers (UK) Ltd
This edition published in 2016 by Bloomsbury Publishing Plc

Bloomsbury Publishing Plc, 50 Bedford Square, London WC1B 3DP

www.bloomsbury.com

Bloomsbury is a trademark of Bloomsbury Publishing Plc

Bloomsbury Publishing, London, New Delhi, New York and Sydney

A catalogue record for this book is available from the British Library

Photographic credits:
John Bailey: 132, 133 (bottom). Howard Bottrell: 26 (background photo), 45, 56, 57 (top), 72 (background photo), 84, 86 (background photo), 92 (background photo), 105 (bottom), 114, 133 (top), 140, 151. Bill Coster: 24, 29, 30 (background photo), 32 (background photo), 37, 59 (background photo), 66, 78 (background photo), 86, 87, 110, 117, 120, 126, 135, 138, 140. Bob Gibbons: 8, 10 (background photo), 21, 36, 44, 47, 54, 59, 60, 61, 65, 76, 77, 78, 79, 105 (top and middle), 112, 113, 115, 116, 122, 128 (background photo), 140 (background photo), 154. imagebroker.net/Photolibrary: 119, 129. istockphoto.com/Stephan Hoerold: 18. istockphoto.com/David Chadwick: 96, 98 (background photo), 148 (background photo). Tim Lucas: 110 (background photo), 114 (background photo). NHPA/Photoshot: 129, 76, 90 (bottom), 128, (top and middle), 137.
Oceans-Image/Photoshot: 72 (bottom), 90 (top), 91. Oxford Scientific/Photolibrary: 127. UPPA/Photoshot:74. Simon Papps: 144. Markus Varesvuo: 111. Woodfall Wild Images/Photolibrary: 72 (top), 73 (top).

All other photographs supplied by the author.

ISBN 978-1-4729-3055-2

Printed in China by RR Donnelley

10 9 8 7 6 5 4 3 2 1

Also available:
Steve Backshall's Deadly 60 (ISBN 978 1 4729 1173 5)
Venom: Poisonous Animals in the Natural World by Steve Backshall (ISBN 978 1 84773 870 7)

CONTENTS

FOREWORD BY MONTY HALLS **7**

INTRODUCTION **8**
The search for adventure 11

THE BASICS **14**
The six S's of wildlife watching 17
Bins and scopes 19
Adventure naturalist's kit 21

FORESTS **24**
Forest magic 27
Birdsong 28
Five birdsongs to know 30
Know your trees 31
Great British trees 32
Marvellous moths 34
Five magnificent moths 36
Getting up high 38
Bug bothering: ten top tips 40
Five beautiful butterflies 44
Mountain biking 48
Building a shelter 50
Five forest finds 52
Woodland tracks and signs 54
Ultimate critter cribs 56
Orchids alive 59
Four fantastic orchids 60
Wild foods: a fungal feast 62
Wild Cooking 64

COAST **66**
Make the most of the coast 69
Rockpooling 70
Rockin' rockpool residents 72
Terrific tides 74
Wading birds: probers and gleaners 75
Seashore tracks and signs 76
Flotsam and jetsam 77
The sandy shore 77
Top finds at the sandy shore 78
Sea kayaking 80
Selected beasties to spot at sea 83
Coasteering 85
Classic coastal critters 86

The underwater world 88
Beautiful bubbles 89
Know your whales 92
Fossil hunting 93
Cooking by the sea 94

MOUNTAINS 96
Magic mountains 99
Navigation 101
Sensing the weather 104
Become a mountain monkey 106
Climbing techniques 108
Remarkable raptors 110
Carnivorous plants of the hills 112
Top fell finds 114
Upland tracks and signs 116
Edible plants of the hills 118

FRESHWATER 120
Watery wonders 123
Pond dipping 123
Amazing aquatic larvae 128
Making wildlife water features 130
Snorkelling in lakes and rivers 131
Freshwater fish 132
Frogwatchin' 134
Riverside tracks and scat 136
Canyoning 138
Caving 139
Five freshwater birds 140
Lighting a fire 142
Free freshwater grub 144

KEEPING RECORDS 146
Records and reminders 149
Using field guides 150
Taking photos 150
Making films 152
What to do with your records 153

FINDING OUT MORE 154
Further reading 156
useful contacts 158

INDEX 159

FOREWORD BY MONTY HALLS

Steve Backshall is really rather annoying. Not only is he younger and fitter than me, he also has more hair and is a very nice chap. Upon meeting Steve it is very difficult to stay annoyed with him for long however, as his enthusiasm and tremendous drive for all things wild and untamed quickly win you over. Steve's lifelong passion for all creatures great and small has taken him to the four corners of the globe, where he has shown a relentless desire to step off the map and seek out things that are truly wild. The man is never happier than when dangling on the end of a rope over some yawning void, crawling through a fetid swamp, hacking through a steaming jungle, or paddling a kayak off a deserted shore – all in the quest to encounter some of the more obscure members of the animal kingdom.

This tremendous energy is backed – happily – by a depth of knowledge that puts the rest of us to shame. It also goes hand in hand with a great respect and affection for all the creatures he encounters – not always the case in the world of modern wildlife film-making. There is also the real weight of knowledge that has been acquired over a lifetime, through trial and error and endless hours at the very coal face of observing animals where they should be seen, in their own habitats. This is the very essence of this splendid book – tips, hints, short cuts and ideas that help the aspiring young naturalist get out there and get on with it.

This is important work. As Steve has amply demonstrated, the young enthusiast of today is the wildlife presenter, the professor, or the conservationist of tomorrow. To fan the spark of an interest in the natural world at an early age is vital, providing the tools to go on to great things later in life. Sadly the legacy of my own generation is destruction, exploitation and the steady eradication of many of the world's natural treasures. We hand over a planet in crisis, with so many ecosystems on the edge of complete destruction. It is the next generation that have the responsibility of arresting the precipitous decline in shark populations, who must rally and defend the remaining tracts of rainforest, develop sustainable tourism, and lobby the great and the good to change the way we regard the delicate ecosystems around us.

My own somewhat erratic career path was fuelled and inspired by the conservation heroes of the age – Jacques Cousteau, Gerald Durrell, and Gavin Maxwell. They showed me that it is possible to make a difference, that by getting out there and getting on with it you can create change. In the modern era I would place Steve amongst the great communicators to the next generation, with his television programmes showing them that there are still wild places, wild creatures, and things worth saving.

This is a wildlife handbook, a technical manual, a reference guide and a thumping good read. To Steve I would say well done on producing a very fine book indeed, with my only complaint being that it wasn't around when I took my own first tentative steps into the wilderness so many years ago. To the reader I would say cram a floppy hat on, throw on a rucksack, and enjoy this book. Use it and trust it – it is your passport to a tremendous world of adventure and knowledge.

INTRODUCTION

Once you get on the road to becoming a naturalist, you are following in the footsteps of some of the boldest explorers to roam the earth, the toughest, most daring discoverers of wonder that ever picked up a magnifying glass.

The search for adventure

I reckon the vast majority of people out there have little or no idea of what a naturalist is or does. Most think it either means you're a weirdo who likes taking off their clothes (that's a naturist by the way), or expect to see an ancient eccentric with a huge beard full of twigs, muttering about Lesser Spotted Warblers. Truth is, The great biologists such as Darwin, Wallace, Humboldt and Bates may have had beards you could hide an orang-utan in, but they were also the first Europeans to set foot in places that'd make a modern explorer's blood run cold! Anyone doubting this should read Wallace's *Malay Archipelago*, one of the greatest adventure yarns ever written. Following in his footsteps through places like New Guinea (remote even today) I've lived with cannibals, found species of animals unknown to science, had to eat countless nasty dishes (the contents of which I still do not want to know), and endured unimaginable discomforts... but he did it over 150 years ago. Back then death or disfigurement from brutal tropical diseases was almost unavoidable, people were still scared that giant many-headed sea monsters would munch their boats, and there was a very real risk that the locals would boil them up in a stew. Wallace is my utter hero, and I would give anything to have been with him on his expeditions.

Even today though, students of the natural world always get to have the best adventures. If you get started early, you could well end up spending your life chasing Chimpanzees through the forests of Tanzania, tagging Lemon Sharks on tropical reefs, maybe ringing Golden Eagles in their lofty Scottish eyries. It all begins here and now, with this book, and the will to get outside and get muddy!

The search for adventure has never been so important. The modern world is very different to when I grew up; there seems to be less space, everyone is in such an almighty hurry all the time, and we're losing touch with what we are, where we come from, and the wonderful world we inhabit. Too many people spend their days in an office typing numbers and figures into a computer, and come home only to plonk themselves in front of the telly. Too many kids actually think they'll be happier playing sports on a games console than going outside and doing it for real. However, I sincerely believe that the hundreds of thousands of years that human beings evolved in the outdoors – with every element of their lives intermingled with nature's rhythms – still has a deep-seated effect on people today. It's instantly obvious on people's faces the first time they get on a horse or a surfboard, the first time they encounter a wild animal, and anytime they're allowed to run feral on a sunshiney day in the country. Young or old, the outdoors, and the animals that live there, make us happy.

This wildlife adventurer's guide is about discovering that wild world, about making the most of the environment we live in (and you can still do that if you live in a big city) about getting fit, getting clued up and getting happy. I also have another motive here, and that's the hope that people who learn to love wildlife and the environment will also be inspired to take care of them.

This guide is laid out habitat by habitat, with sections on the plants and animals you are likely to find in each environment, practical things you can do, and challenges you can undertake. There are sections on equipment, techniques, conservation, tracking, survival

techniques, even country cooking that you can do from nature's free menu. I'm afraid there are also endless warnings of ways you need to take care in order that your adventure in the countryside doesn't turn sour, but I'm telling you now – this book is not a safety blanket, you still need to use your common sense. (That will make my mother laugh; it's taken me a hundred near-death experiences over the years to develop any common sense of my own!)

I'm fully expecting some old-school naturalists to go red in the face with rage when they see some of the things suggested in this book – fell running to see mountain birds? Surfing in order to see seals? Preposterous! Well, for me being an adventure naturalist is about a fundamental turn around in perceptions, and about a whole way of living your life. A birder who sets out to see a Goshawk is more likely to see one than a mountain biker who spends every weekend thundering through Welsh forests. However, if that mountain biker knew what a Goshawk looks and sounds like and was always on the look out for signs while passing through the bird's homeland, I think that balance might change. Once you know a simple birdsong or recognize a common plant, its presence will enlighten even a walk to the shops. Any activity that gets you outside is going to increase your chances of extraordinary wild encounters; doubly so sports such as mountaineering and sea kayaking that can take you to the world's wildest corners.

Naturalists such as Darwin and Wallace looked out on an undiscovered world that was theirs to explore, and their golden age is long past, but there are great miracles to be uncovered right in your local woods or waterways. While some things in the modern world have changed for the worse, there are also many more opportunities if you're just prepared to get out there and give it a go. There are more organizations doing more things in the outdoors than ever before and more activities for you to have a go at. There has never been a better time to get out there, and it has never been more important. I honestly believe people cannot ever be truly happy without discovering the wild world... so get out and have great adventures with wildlife!

◀ *Learning to abseil in the style of the ancient inhabitants of St Kilda; barefoot and with a hemp rope... though of course they didn't have fancy modern helmets!*

The Basics

of smell at least 10,000 times better than a human, and there is evidence that bears and even pigs may be even more sensitive. When out on the Arctic tundra tracking Polar Bear, we spotted a bear perhaps two miles away, just in time to see him lift his nose, clearly scent us on the air and shamble off into the distance. Just a whiff of you or your artificial fragrances will send sensitive animals running. Another thing to think about in the stink category is yet another 'S': stay downwind of any wildlife you want to observe – so the wind is blowing from it to you rather than vice-versa. Toss a small piece of grass into the air and note which way it floats away – you want to be approaching any animals from that direction (i.e. downwind) when stalking. It's a tricky one, this, and not one you often get the chance to use in practice, but useful if you're thinking of placing a hide, or staking out a potential food source. From experience though, I can tell you that if you do spend hours putting up a hide downwind of a surefire viewing site, the wind will change just as you apply the finishing touches…

SIGHT

The way you use your eyes is actually something you can improve. I personally find searching for animals at night easier than in the daytime, not just because there's more out and about, but because the beam of a torch concentrates the vision, and cuts out extraneous information. Another essential bit of kit that can do the same thing for you is a pair of binoculars or spotting scope.

▲ *Don't forget a torch if you're out at night!*

SCAT

I could have called this by another 'S', but referring to droppings, faeces – good old fashioned poo – as 'scat' helps you to get rid of squeamishness and feel like a scientist or expert native tracker. I've managed to so completely get over any worries about the brown stuff that I often find myself taking appropriate pieces apart in my fingers and shoving it under my nose for a good sniff – I have to admit I've even had a wee taste of Black Bear scat (in late summer their diet is so catholic that it tastes like blueberry pie!). There are several sections throughout this guide that should help you to basically differentiate the scat from broad animal groups, tell how fresh it is, and a little of what the depositor was feeding on. But please wear gloves or at least wash your hands after handling scat, and don't eat it – I get paid to do this stuff and can afford an occasional case of the trots!

Bins and scopes

When you think about getting your first pair of binoculars, it can be a little confusing – lots of weird numbers and scary differences in prices. Hopefully this explanation will make things a little clearer, but as your bins will be your most important piece of kit as a naturalist, it's important to think about it carefully and get the best you can afford.

Typically, the optics of a set of bins will be described with two numbers, for example 8 x 40. The first number is the magnification; in this case your view will be enlarged eight times beyond what you would see through your own eyes.

The second number is the diameter of the objective (large) lens in millimetres – in this case, 40 mm. The larger this lens is, the more light can get in. So it might seem a set of 20 x 70 mm bins would be the ideal... but bins to this spec are huge, which makes them a nightmare to lug around and hold steady. As an adventure naturalist, you need to get a good pay off between size and weight and performance. Waterproofing is also something I can't do without, as mine live with me, even in the sea kayak. I have a pair of 8 x 40 Swarovskis, and am utterly in love with them, as they seem to work brilliantly in every situation.

If you intend to do a lot of watching from hides, a telescope (or 'spotting scope') on a tripod will provide much higher magnifying power for prolonged scans of wide vistas – many scopes come with up to 60 mm zoom eyepieces. However, such setups are cumbersome to lug about if you're walking any distance or tackling rough terrain.

SIGN

There is absolutely nothing to make you feel more like a master of your environment than finding a few footprints in the sand, stroking your chin in contemplation and surmising, 'Fallow Deer, a mother and fawn, here within the last hour and moving off in a westerly direction.' Of course, you're almost certain to then round a corner and meet the sheep that actually made the prints (probably eating your sandwiches), but eventually you'll get some predictions right, and feel like a tracking mystic. The most important part of tracking is not actually your recognition of the sign itself, but of spotting substrates (that means types of material that things live or grow on) that will best hold a print. A classic example would be the clear muddy sides of a river with worn animal 'roads' leading away over the banks, or obvious woodland trails after fresh snowfall. Once you've sussed what kind of animal

▲ Although it's not British, I just had to include this Brown Bear print. We followed the tracks around a snowy lakeshore until we came face to face with the bear herself, hunting salmon in the shallows.

made the tracks, their gait and type of movement is easy to assess, by putting yourself almost literally into their shoes.

Adventure naturalist's kit

I was a cub scout and I believe in always being prepared. Besides the crucial binoculars, there are certain items that an adventurer is often going to need — get into the habit of carrying the smaller things around, as they're no use to you in a drawer at home. Specific wildlife-catching tools are covered in the relevant sections, the following is just general stuff.

HAND LENS

More useful than a magnifying glass, as hand lenses fold up nice and small, and can have much higher magnification. These are great for examining close-up detail on an insect's body, and usually come in strengths of x5 to x20 magnification. It's not a bad idea to have a selection.

The technique to seeing through it well is to control the lens close to your eye, and move the object you're studying until it's in focus, rather than trying to focus by moving the lens around. Such lenses can also be used to start a fire in a survival situation.

KNIFE

Use great caution and common sense here; after all it's illegal and dangerous to carry a knife on the streets these days. Go for a nice, small Swiss Army knife, and only carry it in your pack when you're out in the wilds. Lock knives should be treated with extreme respect, as cheaper models may well spring shut even while locked – and potentially take off your fingers! Moving up the scale, a machete is an essential survival tool when you really are far from the beaten track, and will help you make shelter, fire and find a meal, but you are not going to need one of these unless you are in a serious survival situation, which is unlikely to occur anywhere in the UK.

POTS AND STUFF

Inevitably whilst you're out wandering you're going to want to pick up stuff like owl pellets, feathers, discarded hair, prey remains and so on, to examine or identify. A good selection of test tubes, pots with lids and manipulating kit such as long tweezers is invaluable, though you should put objects back where you found them after you've checked them out.

MICROSCOPE

You're not going to be dragging this around in the field, and they're pricey as well as rather bulky, so I'll not put too much into talking about it. However, a microscope can be a great window on a hidden tiny world, and a fabulous way of learning about how things work, by examining their tiny details. The important number to focus on is the magnification; most microscopes will have a revolving set of lenses with a selection of different magnifications. You can also get very reasonable USB microscopes that plug into your computer, which are great little toys!

FIELD GUIDES

It doesn't matter how advanced you are as a naturalist, you can never know everything, and even the world's greatest experts still have a good collection of field guides. I personally live with a whole bunch of them in the back of my car, so if I find an obscure species of invertebrate I've never seen before, I can at least attempt to identify it as soon as possible. As a starter I'd highly recommend something like Collins' *Complete British Wildlife*, and when cash allows start buying guides to different groups.

NOTEBOOK

Unless you have a team of Sherpas, it's impossible to carry round a collection of reference material comprehensive enough to enable you to identify everything you find. That's why you should always carry a notebook, so you can record your impressions on the ground rather than trying to commit the details of a fleetingly seen animal to memory and attempting to identify it later.

Practice making notes and field sketches on the spot of animals you know well, and you'll be better prepared when you encounter something new. It's also nice to make general notes about your adventures – you can relive them later to brighten up a less interesting day. Choose a notebook that will fit in your pocket, with a sturdy binding that will stand up to a bit of rain and general abuse. What to write with? Pens can run out of ink, pencils can snap and smudge and both are easy to lose – you're probably best off carrying at least one of each.

SURVIVAL KIT

It's always wise to carry a selection of handy bits and pieces for emergencies. I used to keep mine in an old tobacco tin, until I got so much in there I couldn't get the darn thing shut! This is something you'll build on as you get more experienced, but to begin with I'd suggest some string, fish hooks, waterproof matches, hand lens, whistle, button compass, mirror, scalpel blades, wire saw, superglue (my all-purpose med kit!) and tweezers. Taking your mobile phone with you can save the day if you get lost – but don't forget to turn off the ring tone if you're in 'stealth mode'. The rest is down to improvisation!

CAMERA

Nowadays even the camera on the average mobile phone is enough to get you some super wildlife photos, and phones have the undeniable advantage of being in your pocket the whole time. The digital age being upon us, I can see precious few reasons to use print film.

Digital photography allows you to monitor your images as you take them and improve your photography far more quickly, as well as allowing you to photograph unfamiliar plants and animals and identify them as soon as you get home rather than waiting for a film to come back from the processors. I'll deal with this more fully in the section on photography, but there is great merit in the new version of the old adage; 'leave nothing but footprints, take nothing but photographs'.

OUTDOOR CLOTHING

Take some time to choose the right clothes for what you want to do, and you'll be much more comfortable out in the field. Plenty of specialist retailers sell outdoor gear and it doesn't have to cost the earth. Army surplus clothing is ideal for staying comfy and inconspicuous. In general, sturdy, water-resistant footwear is a must. For clothes, choose tough, breathable fabrics in dull greens, browns or camouflage patterns. It's useful to pick trousers/shorts and tops with lots of pockets for your various bits and pieces.

When choosing clothes in shops, try the 'swish test' – walk around and see how much noise the fabric makes as you move. There's no point picking beautifully camouflaged gear if you sound like an approaching hurricane. If you are going to be out and about in hot weather you'll need a hat to protect your head from sunburn (as well as sunblock of course), while cold weather demands warm headgear (perhaps with ear flaps), and layered clothing with a windproof outer 'shell'. Mountaineers are fond of saying 'there's no such thing as bad weather, only bad clothing'. Certainly, modern materials are your best defence against both hypothermia (getting superchilled) and hyperthermia (overheating). I've had both several times, it's extremely frightening and both can be life-threatening, even in Britain's apparently modest climate. Long sleeves and trousers will help protect you from thorny foliage and biting insects, and Wellington boots are useful when exploring boggy or coastal environments.

▶ All-weather gear that can keep the elements at bay sometimes has to be more important than camouflage – particularly when sea kayaking amongst ice floes as I was here!

FORESTS

At one time, almost all of the British Isles was covered with ancient forests of huge craggy oaks, elms and beech trees carpeted with moss, and inhabited by Brown Bears, Wolves and Wild Boar. Even today, some of the most mystical, enchanted places in the world can be found in good old-fashioned British woods.

Forest magic

The vast majority of that wonderful wilderness has been lost to the chainsaws, crops and cities of modern man, but there are still places where you can experience the magic of how our nation once was; and perhaps feel like a modern day Robin Hood while you're at it. However, as in forests all over the world, the amount of plant life can give the animals an endless amount of places to hide, so in order to maximize your chances of seeing anything, there's a whole heap of tricks you can do to make the wildlife come to you.

Standing in the lush green cavern of a typical European forest in summer, sunlight slanting down through the foliage in golden shafts, it's easy to feel enclosed, claustrophobic, almost overpowered by the amount of life about you. However, plant life needs light to thrive, and the majority of plant growth is actually going on way above your head in the canopy. Up here, Purple Hairstreak butterflies flit amongst oak leaves, evading the attentions of hunting flycatchers. Goldfinch chicks fledge from nests woven through with gossamer stolen from spider's webs, and Hazel Dormice spend the majority of their days in blissful slumber, only emerging from their treetop holes on fine evenings.

Descending through the leaves and branches, we reach the understorey. Here, younger trees and shrubs jostle for light, Grey Squirrels chatter at intruders from their messy dreys with a sound like a child imitating a machine gun, occasionally making a wailing spoilt-baby 'waaah' sound to warn off other squirrels. At ground level there are grasses, ferns, brambles and herbaceous plants, and then the leaf litter – the best place to go looking for exciting invertebrates. For me, the highlights of a forest environment are always the small things, animals that are nowadays known as minibeasts. There are different species found at all levels of the forest, from the ground to the canopy, and lots of different ways to make these sometimes shy beasties show themselves.

As the forest is a place of plenty for wildlife, so it offers everything a modern adventurer could need to survive. A basic knowledge of some edible wild plants and fungi, ways to cook your wild fare, and a few types of shelter are all dealt with here.

Birdsong

One of the most satisfying of skills for a naturalist to learn is identifying birds by their songs and calls. Once this was only achievable through long years of experience, but thanks to the advent of the MP3 player, and a profusion of different CDs of birdsong, anyone can learn a few basic calls. Knowing that my ability to identify birdsong was sadly lacking, I downloaded a whole bunch of these, and listened to little or nothing else for a year. Now I can tell if a Sparrowhawk, Fox, owl or cat is nearby by the strident warnings of the songbirds, can pick out a young male bird trying to set up a territory from his bold advertising song, and even hear the birds commenting on me as I pass by. It has made a huge impact on how much I can enjoy a simple stroll in the woods, even on the days I don't actually see anything.

Songs are, however, incredibly complex. A Blackbird for example may give a song and a subsong (a quieter, less structured version of the full song, often performed through partially shut bill), and may, like other thrushes, mimic the songs of other birds. They also have several different alarm, startle and contact calls. That's a whole avian language for you to learn, and that's just one species! However, the father of a friend of mine worked his whole life as a gamekeeper, and could tell the age of a bird, and even whether it was embarking on the first, second or third brood of the season, without needing to see it – all from listening carefully to the song. As this is such an immense subject, it's best to get started on it right now.

TALK TO THE ANIMALS

This is a wonderful way of interacting with wildlife, and of getting birds closer to you. However, it should be used with caution, particularly during breeding seasons, when you may be distracting birds from their jobs at the most important time of the year.

One of the easiest bird songs to recognize is the two-note call of the Cuckoo, which sounds like... well, like; 'cuckoo, cuckoo'! When you hear this song nearby, try mimicking it through clasped hands. This may well bring the bird closer to check you out. There are several cheap bird call imitators on the market that will have even better results. One of the best is a Tawny Owl whistle, which will give you a near perfect owl call.

The best way to try one out is to go out in the early evening, and listen out for the call of a nearby Tawny. You may hear two distinct phrases – a sharp *keewick* and the low fluty *hooowooo* hoot, the archetypal owl song. The two sounds are made by two different owls. The former is a contact call (effectively, 'Is anyone there?') and the latter is the male's territorial hoot, given in response ('Yes, me!'). If you can perfect your own *hooowooo*, our most common owl may well come super close to investigate the intruder.

'Pishing' is a weird name for an even weirder birder's trick. Don't get caught doing this in public, it's the sort of thing that could get you arrested! It's simple in theory, just make lots of loud 'pish pish pish' noises, or perhaps loud squeaky kissing of the back of your hand. Tongue clicks also work for sparrows. Nearby birds may

◀ The Tawny Owl is more often heard than seen.

The Great Tit's song is rich and varied, which can make it difficult to identify.

take the high sibilant sounds to be the alarm calls of other birds, or the squeaks of Stoats or Weasels, and come in close to look at the source of the sounds. The chances of success is affected by the time of year, the proximity of the right sort of birds (small songbirds respond best) and even how much pishing you've done in the area recently.

So why would small birds, potentially prey species, turn up to investigate a threat and maybe turn themselves into lunch? Well, it's probably for the exact same reason that, when you see a bird of prey, it's often being mobbed by a much smaller bird. Birds gang up to try and drive away those that might harm them or their offspring, and genuinely appear to have more guts than anything many times their size.

Five birdsongs to know

CHAFFINCH This is a very common bird and its song, with a characteristic 'waterfall' feel and downwards flourish at the end, is perhaps the easiest of tunes to learn – not to be confused with the slower-paced song of the less common Willow Warbler.

ROBIN This wistful tune just says Britain! It's highly pitched and much thinner than that of the Wren or thrushes, with slow notes but also lots of garbled phrases, perhaps sounding a little like someone who's struggling to whistle a complicated tune.

WREN One of our smallest birds, this species has one of the biggest voices. It's often said that if you can hear a song that appears almost too loud and too penetrating, look hard enough and you'll see this tiny bird with its characteristic upturned tail.

BLACKBIRD My favourite birdsong, I could listen to this beautiful, powerful, crystal-clear fluted warble for hours. You know this song already, I guarantee it, and just need to watch a Blackbird in voice to associate it with the bird. The *chink chink chink* alarm call is one I hear non-stop throughout the spring, as my neighbours have hungry cats! Blackbirds, like Mistle and Song Thrushes, may mimic sounds they hear in their songs.

GREAT TIT Celebrated bird boffin Bill Oddie claims that if you hear a birdcall you can't identify, it's probably a Great Tit! Its song is typically a repetitious two-note *teacher teacher teache*r, but this little bird has so many calls and song variants that it can always cause confusion. The usual alarm call is a sort of hollow rattling noise.

Know your trees

It's one of the first lessons every kid learns in school, the basic tree types found regularly in British countryside. However, it's so basic that often it's knowledge that we forget to revise or develop (and let's face it – most of us just forget it). It's essential though, as the nooks, crannies, branches and bounty of each individual tree creates a unique environment, that (in the case of the oaks for example) may harbour as many as 400 animal species. Some species are so closely connected to one kind of tree that they're not found anywhere else. The glorious Sycamore Moth caterpillar with its punky orange haircut, the Oak Bush-cricket sporting a scimitar-shaped ovipositor, the magnificent Lime Hawkmoth, gall wasps that only lay their eggs in particular tree species... you could write an entire book about the insects whose lives are inexorably intertwined with any one kind of tree.

Broadly speaking, there are two different types of tree:

DECIDUOUS. These are the trees that shed their leaves, usually in autumn. Most familiar trees native to Britain are deciduous broad-leaved trees which produce flowers and fruit.
EVERGREEN. These trees have leaves all year round. Most evergreen trees in Britain are coniferous and have thin and waxy leaves (think of the needles on a Christmas tree). They don't produce flowers. Instead, their pollen and seeds are produced in cones. Most conifers in Britain are introduced species.

▲ Like most trees native to Britain, the imposing English Oak loses its leaves each year.

▲ The evergreen Scots Pine is one of only three conifers native to Britain.

Great British trees

ELM There are several different types of elm here in the UK, up to about 30 m tall with a broad, rounded crown to the tree. The leaves are arranged along  each twig alternately, and are kind of eye-shaped. Unfortunately, one of the things this tree is best known for is the blight of Dutch Elm disease, which devastated elms throughout the 20th century.

MOUNTAIN ASH Also known as Rowan, this is a fast grower in the rose family  that is generally smaller than the other deciduous trees mentioned here, rarely exceeding 20 m. The leaflets are thin ovals with teeth along the edges, held together in regular side-by-side arrangements that turn a beautiful red in autumn. In early summer they produce bunches of white flowers, and by late summer dense bunches of orange or red berries appear.

LIME Unrelated to the citrus of the the same name, these large trees grow to about 34 m tall. The leaves are like plump hearts, with soft hairs on either side. When the  tree is in bloom it has a delightful fragrance. The bark is grey with shallow vertical indentations, and the inner bark has been used over the years as rope and for weaving things like baskets. These trees suffer quite badly from infestations by aphids. Don't leave your car or tent underneath a lime tree in the summer, as it will end up sticky with honeydew excreted by the insects feeding above.

SYCAMORE Well known for their clustered seeds, which 'helicopter' down to the ground. They're in the maple family, so to remember the leaf shape, just think of the Canadian flag: hand-shaped, with three large lobes pointing up and out, and two smaller ones near the leafstalk.

BEECH The Common Beech is an especially familiar sight on the chalky soils of southern England, in mixed deciduous woodlands but often

also as a virtual monoculture. Because the trees form such a tight canopy, almost nothing grows at ground level inside a Common Beech woodland, giving it an eerie cavelike feeling! The best way of identifying this species is by its plump oval leaves, comparatively smooth bark and the autumn nutlets (beechmast) with their triangular cross-section and four-lobed hairy husk.

OAK We have a variety of different oak species in the UK, but

most common are the Sessile and English Oaks. Both sport the familiar lobed leaves, and produce acorns in the autumn. Old oaks can be huge and reach 40m, and while a lifespan of several centuries is expected, a few examples have lived for over 1,000 years.

SWEET CHESTNUT The large leaves are clustered together in groups, and each is edged with bristly teeth. The tree itself has a broad crown and may appear expansive and squat. The fruit, enclosed in needle-covered casings, is the chestnut we commonly roast over an open fire.

Marvellous moths

I can hear you thinking as you read this: 'Why on earth would we want to bother with moths? They're dull, ugly night-monsters that munch our clothes.' Well, this couldn't be further from the truth; actually many of our native moths are more colourful than their butterfly counterparts, there are more species of day-flying moths than day-flying butterflies, and only a very few species will chew through our jumpers! Trust me, few butterflies in Britain can beat the impressiveness of some of our hawkmoths, the bright colours of the tiger moths or the Cinnabar and the camouflage of such species as the Buff Tip or Mottled Beauty.

MOTH TRAPS

There's a variety of suggested reasons for why lights attract moths. Perhaps the best is that they navigate by keeping a set angle between themselves and the moon. As the moon is so far away, it appears to stay at the same position in the sky as they travel. However, big lights con the moths, and they start trying to navigate by keeping these at a set angle away from themselves. This means they get closer and closer to the light and eventually fly straight into it. Imagine if you were in a car heading down a straight road and the moon was directly in front of you – it would appear to stay there. If you were driving down the same road trying to keep a street lamp in front of you, you'd eventually drive into it.

The best kind of light to use for a moth trap emits ultraviolet light, as insects see way better in those wavelengths of light (if you look at flowers under ultraviolet light, the petals show beautiful markings that we can't see, but pollinating bees can). Shining a UV torch onto a hung white sheet works wonders.

Even more dramatic in its results is the mercury vapour trap. These consist of a box, with a powerful UV lamp in the centre. They can be powered with batteries, portable generators or from the mains. The moths gather around the lamp and fall inside the box, where they can be examined at your leisure. Place something in the box for the moths to rest on (broken-up egg boxes work well), and make sure you release all your captures at the place they were found. If you let them go the next day, be aware that some moths are very reluctant to fly in the daytime and so can be difficult to 'release' – if they don't want to fly away, carefully place them in sheltered spots where they won't be easily detected by predators.

Moths, clockwise from bottom left: Eyed Hawkmoth, Burnished Brass, Peppered, Brimstone, Magpie, August Thorn, Hummingbird Hawkmoth

MOTH MIX

Though many moths don't feed at all as adults, others will gorge themselves at night from nectar-rich flowers such as honeysuckle.

Moth mix makes the most of the moths' amazing s u p e r - t u n e d sense of smell to attract them in for a feed.

Note that moth mix will not work that well in the summer, when there are so many plants in the woods with their own endless sources of nectar that moths have an embarrassment of riches.

▲ *Contrary to popular opinion, moths don't just come out at night. The two impressive beasties enjoying a spot of sun here are Poplar Hawkmoths.*

To make your moth mix, take some brown sugar, molasses, a little red wine or beer, and boil it all up in a big pot. You'll end up with a sweet, sickly fluid which smells absolutely divine – but don't drink it, it's potent stuff! Paint this mix onto trees and fenceposts – my expert naturalist comrade Nick Baker suggests dunking an old pair of socks in the moth mix and hanging them from a washing line – and come back some hours later to see if you've got any results. (I suspect if I were to use some of my old socks, the only result would be a bunch of dead moths.)

While your light trap or moth mix is at work, cast your torch around nearby branches. Moths have a layer of shiny material at the back of their eyes that reflects light to improve their night vision. This gives off a ghostly glow when your torch glances off it, and you may be able to get close and examine them.

Five magnificent moths

SWALLOWTAILED MOTH Certainly one of our prettiest moths, the Swallowtailed Moth flies in late June and July. It's often found at dusk and early evenings in woodlands, and is also seen in gardens and commons, as long as the twig-like caterpillars have plenty to feed on. They're partial to ivy, elder, hawthorn and blackthorn, and will also munch on many other shrubs.

FIVE-SPOT BURNET The various burnets and the Cinnabar blow every myth about moths out of the water. They're brightly coloured, with a party frock of black and red polka dots. The burnets have club-shaped antennae like butterflies, and they're only active during the day. You'll most likely see them wandering over flowers in damp terrain such as marshes and meadows.

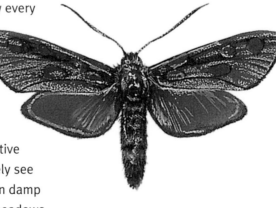

HUMMINGBIRD HAWKMOTH The first time I saw one of these, a pal was screaming at me: 'Look, look, a hummingbird on that bush!' Thousands of people are likewise conned every summer, when these extraordinary creatures migrate to British shores. They hover in front of nectar-rich flowers, dipping their long proboscis into each bloom in turn to lap up the sweet nectar.

MOTHER OF PEARL An exquisite little moth, with wings seemingly pressed from liquid mother of pearl. This is one of the many Lepidoptera (smart name for moths and butterflies) species whose caterpillars make their homes rolled up in nettle leaves, which makes this a great place to go looking for them! You can also find caterpillars of Small Tortoiseshell, Comma, Peacock and Red Admiral butterflies feeding in nettles.

PINE PROCESSIONARY This is one moth that nobody wanted to make its way to the UK. However, it has come across from warmer parts of Europe, and although it's rare to see processionary moths in Britain, they are probably here to stay. The caterpillars make silken nests during the day high up in pine trees, then at night head out in snakelike head-to-toe processions looking for food. These moths are so unpopular because the caterpillars' nasty hairs can irritate anyone who gets too close, causing respiratory problems, dermatitis and even temporary blindness. Last time I went to Kew Gardens, there was paint splashed on all the trees that had been infested with a related moth, the Oak Processionary, which had arrived from Europe, possibly in imported timber. Kew scientists are investigating the moths in the lab in the hope that they will discover a way of controlling them and preventing their spread to other areas.

Getting up high

The most exciting environment in a forest is up in the highest branches of the biggest trees, where you can truly get a bird's eye view of what's going on. As a kid, climbing trees was something my friends and I did every day, getting way up into the canopy without using ropes at all. Nowadays, such a potentially dangerous pastime shouldn't be encouraged. Luckily, all around the country outdoor centres are starting to build rope courses that allow people to get safely up into the treetops.

ROPEWORK

Modern canopy ropework involves getting two ropes up and into the highest branches of big trees, then ascending on bits of equipment that grip the rope. Once you're adept at the technique, a tree can be rigged in about half an hour, and climbed in safety in just a minute or two – well, depending on the size of course. Some of the rainforest giants I've been lucky enough to climb have been over 80 m high, and when it's hot and humid, that feels like a very long way.

Do not attempt to put the ropework technique into practice without training and supervision from suitably experienced and qualified people – this is dangerous stuff and you'll need specialist knowledge as well as a head for heights. First, the tree needs to be carefully vetted, checked for signs of rot or disease, and a suitably sturdy branch needs to be selected. Then a catapult, bow or crossbow is used to fire a weight with a line attached over the branch. This may seem like the fun bit – particularly when you're firing arrows into a tree or using a catapult bigger than yourself, but it is also the most difficult bit, and can take up lots of time if you keep missing. With a thin guiding line in place over a suitable bough, two thicker ropes are dragged up over the branch and then back down to the ground where they are tied off to another, sturdy tree. The strength of the lines must be tested with the weight of at least two people before anyone begins the climb.

Several firms around the UK have courses that will teach you the techniques of canopy ropework, and even industrial qualifications that could lead to work as a tree surgeon – perhaps the perfect occupation for an adventure naturalist, although one of the most dangerous jobs in the world.

this is dangerous stuff and you'll need specialist knowledge

Bug bothering: ten top tips

Woodlands, forests, even parks and gardens that have trees and large bushes, are the best places in the country to go looking for creepy-crawlies. If you're a little squeamish about bugs, consider that the whole world would work just fine without all of its mammals and birds, but take away all the invertebrates and within weeks our ecosystems would shut down. Also, whilst there are maybe 5,000 or 5,500 species of mammals worldwide, there are unknown millions of insects. Nobody could ever know everything about this astounding group of creatures.

Remember, these are living things and deserve as much consideration and respect as any other. If you catch them, handle them with exquisite care and let them go where you found them as soon as possible. If you can observe them without interfering in their lives at all, so much the better.

STICK-SHAKING

This is as basic – and as much fun– as it sounds! Get yourself a big white sheet (it needs to be white so all the critters show up on it), and lay it or ask some pals to hold it underneath a bush, hedge, or the branches of a low-hanging tree. Then you take a big stick, slide it carefully into the foliage and give it a short, sharp shake. Most insects have grippy little

▲ You're bound to see a whole variety of creepy crawlies if you try this bug-collecting technique.

feet equipped with spiky claws that'll help them hang on to just about anything. However, if you catch them by surprise, they'll fall into the sheet and then you can set about examining them. This method works very well in conjunction with the pooter.

PITFALL TRAPS

The pitfall trap is the first bit of kit for any field entomologist (that's a bug scientist to you and me) worth their salt. Basically, it's just any deepish container, sunk into the ground, with the lip of the trap flush with the soil. Inattentive passing minibeasts will simply fall into the trap. You can place bait in the bottom, and a few chunks of wood or leaves so nervous bugs have somewhere to shelter. Very important is a small hole in the bottom of the trap so rainwater will run away and not drown anything inside. These traps are a perfect way to suss out which invertebrates are living in the leaf litter, but MUST be checked regularly, and never left in place for long periods of time. I have caught frogs, lizards and even tiny shrews inside some of my larger traps, and it would be awful if any animal died of starvation or exposure because you hadn't checked your traps. Basically, pitfallin' is a technique to experiment with. You can use traps the size of buckets or even dustbins, but disposable plastic coffee cups can also get results. Placing bait in the bottom of the trap works, as does placing it on a stick over the top of the trap, or hanging from a wigwam of sticks above it. A bit of mushy, stinky banana will attract ground beetles, millipedes and ants, some oats will attract weevils and other beetles, a bit of poo (up to you where you get it from...) may attract the fascinating dung beetles that we have in the UK – and probably a fly or two!

SWEEP NETTING

This is old-school Victorian-style bug collection, although it's hopefully moved on a bit since then; the Victorians used to kill and pin everything they caught, and that's not cool in the 21st century. What you're going to need is a good old-fashioned butterfly net (available from any natural history supplies website), though it's not just for butterflies. A good method for catching an array of bugs is to find a meadow of long grasses (particularly in the spring or summer) and walk through it, briskly sweeping the net through the tops of the grasses. You'll catch an array of micromoths, grasshoppers and bush crickets, probably a ladybird or two. Handle everything you capture with extreme care, taking special care not to handle delicate wings. More precise netting is generally reserved for butterflies. Try and sweep them up from behind gently, examine and identify them from a gently gathered bunch of netting, and release them as soon as possible. Rough handling will rub off the colourful scales that cover the wings (without them the wings are totally transparent), removing camouflage that protects them from predators, and the colours that make them attractive to a mate. Many scarce species of insects are protected by law from any kind of disturbance, so err on the side of caution at all times.

POOTER

The pooter is a simple device that allows you to catch insects through the power of suction so that you can get a closer look at them, and needs to be used in conjunction with good bug-finding techniques. You can't beat turning over rotten logs in your local woods to find exciting beetles, centipedes and millipedes. To make the pooter, you'll need a jar with a plastic lid, about a foot of plastic tubing, and a small piece of very fine fabric. Cut or burn two holes in the plastic lid at the same diameter as the tubing. Then cut one short piece of tube (this is the end that you'll suck), and leave one longer. Push each through a hole in the lid. Next you will need to secure the fine fabric over the end of the sucking-in tube that will be inside the collecting jar. Make sure this is well secured with an elastic band. When you find an insect, place the long tube over it and suck through the sucking-in tube – the insect should be sucked into the jar but the fabric seal will make sure it goes no further. Be careful not to suck up creatures with fragile spindly legs as they may break, and no slugs and snails unless you want your pooter all gooey! Be warned though – when pootering there is no insuring against pranksters. On one of my filming shoots, the cameraman sneakily removed the fabric from the pooter, and one of the young lads out bug-hunting managed to actually inhale a woodlouse. It nearly choked him!

THE TULGREN FUNNEL

This is a great way of finding the tiny animals that live in the undergrowth. Take a plastic funnel, and place it into a collection pot of some kind – a jam jar would work fine. Then take a few good handfuls of dead leaf litter from your local woods, and put them into the funnel. Next you need to place a desk lamp inches away from the leaf litter (but not so close that it sets fire to the leaves). The minibeasts that inhabit the dark, damp leaf litter will try and get as far away from the light and its warmth as possible, and a few hours later, your collecting pot should be alive with tiny beasties. A magnifying glass or hand lens will help you to identify and get a closer look at whatever you find.

CATERPILLAR CATCHING

One of the only crystal-clear memories I have from when I was five years old was the first time I saw a butterfly emerging from its chrysalis. It was in my school classroom, and had the whole class gathered around gasping in awe and wonder. Having spent much of the rest of my life travelling and seeing the world's most spectacular animals, it remains an unbeatable spectacle, yet it is something anyone can replicate in their own home. The simple way to do this is to go out for a country walk and look in as many plants as possible for caterpillars or even, if you are really lucky, eggs fixed to the underside of a leaf (often looking like little bunches of yellow Tic Tacs). Make sure you identify the species before you take them home – only attempt to rear common species at home and leave the rest where you found them.

Take the eggs or caterpillars and lots of the plant you found them on, so they'll have some food. Place the plants in water on your windowsill, and watch the caterpillars munch their way through the leaves. A gentle mist spray of water every few days will help keep proceedings moist. If you're at all worried the caterpillars are not doing very well, return them to where you found them straight away.

The larvae will moult and grow, shedding their skins several times before they start to pupate. Some moths need to bury down into the soil to do this, so you'll need to have made an attempt at identifying your caterpillars, and if they appear to be moths, house your plant in soil about 20 cm deep. Many butterflies hang their chrysalis from a twig. Inside this seemingly dead casing, amazing changes are taking place. Make sure this pupa is kept in a cool place; it could be a few weeks or even months before the adult emerges. Again this is when having had a crack at identifying the caterpillar will help, as each species pupates for a different amount of time – some overwinter as pupae and emerge in the spring.

SNAIL STEW

Right, now you're going to have quite a job convincing people that it's a good idea to attract slugs and snails. After all, these are the enemies of every gardener. However, I have a few good reasons why you should want to watch these magical little critters in action. Firstly, slug and snail locomotion is utterly fascinating. They secrete goo which runs down channels in their body to the foot, where it's used to lubricate their progress across your lawn. Secondly, this method allows you to see their way of feeding, grinding food up with a rasping tongue called a radula. Thirdly, once you've summoned slugs and snails to one spot to feed, they can be easily collected, and released in local woodlands away from your cabbages! The way to attract them is to make up a slug stew: chunks of lettuce and apples, mixed with a little water and some sugar in a blender. Take the nasty green goo this creates, and paint it onto some panes of glass which can then be placed in your vegetable patch (or wherever you most often get slugs and snails). Looking at them from the other side of the glass, you'll be able to properly examine them feeding. Be careful when handling any slugs or snails, and remember that salt will dry up or dessicate them – much better to release them elsewhere, or encourage a hedgehog to make its home in your garden (they love munching slugs and snails).

EARWIG HOME

The first time I tried this, I was working on the Springwatch farm for the BBC, and put together an earwig home, thoroughly sceptical about the chances of it working. The next day when I tested the results live on camera, there were so many earwigs inside that I was totally convinced the production team had set it all up while I wasn't watching. However, having tried it again since, it clearly just works really well! Take a flower pot, and fill it up with straw. Then pour lots of gooey honey into the straw, and whack a piece of bamboo cane or wooden spoon into the flower pot to fix it in place. Turn it upside down (without tipping honey-covered straw out everywhere) and plant the cane or spoon handle into the ground, particularly at the edges of a lawn or near to dense vegetation. Earwigs are 'thigmotropic' and like many invertebrates they love to stay in enclosed places. They'll be attracted by the sweet honey, then find a whole bunch of places inside the straw where they can make a squeezed-in home. If you're wondering why you should be interested in earwigs, they are among the best parents of all insects. Each female broods her eggs, tends and even feeds her young until they are old enough to take care of themselves.

BEE BOXES

Bees are some of the most loved of all garden residents as they help to pollinate your flowers, and there's a whole variety of ways you can attract them to make their home near to you. A bumblebee home is quite similar to the earwig one described above: take a flowerpot, put in a little straw, then place it upside down on a paving slab or step, with a little gap left to allow the bees to get inside. Apparently, if you find a disused wild mouse nest, and use the bedding from that, the chance of bees taking up residence is almost 100 per cent. Bumblebees make their homes in old mouse nests in the wild, and are attracted to the smell. To attract other kinds of bees, as well as lacewings and ladybirds that'll munch down aphids off your roses, simply take a box with one face missing – or you could use a flowerpot again. Then fill this

Five beautiful butterflies

SWALLOWTAIL Perhaps our most dramatic butterfly, with lurid yellow, blue and black patterns, as well as a vibrant red eyespot on the hindwing. In the UK they only breed in the Norfolk Broads, though migrants from the continent are occasionally seen elsewhere, especially on the south coast of England. The caterpillars feed only on Milk Parsley. This species' rarity is such that it enjoys full legal protection and its caterpillars and eggs must never be taken from the wild.

COMMON BLUE There is a plethora of different blue butterflies found throughout the UK, and they are difficult to tell apart. The commonest species are the Common Blue (in meadows and downland) and the Holly Blue, which is more slivery on the underwings, lacks the big orange spots of the Common Blue and is more likely in woods and gardens. In all other situations, boldly state: 'That's a Common Blue' and hope to goodness no one else knows better!

Along with other blues, the caterpillar secretes honeydew, which makes it attractive to ants. In return for this nutrient-rich reward, the ants protect the caterpillar (and possibly the chrysalis too) from predators.

PEARL-BORDERED FRITILLARY
This small, rare fritillary has the golden, black-spotted upperwings typical of its family, and when seen from underneath is a startlingly intricate and delicately patterned little beauty. It flies through the early summer, usually has only one brood, and its caterpillars feed on different types of wild violets. The related Small Pearl-bordered Fritillary is distressingly similar – check the underwings to tell them apart.

GATEKEEPER One of the 'browns', which are also numerous and difficult to differentiate. You'll recognize the Gatekeeper by the black eyespot on the top of the forewing, with two white dots inside it. These gold-and-brown butterflies are commonly found around brambles, and will show signs of being territorial if other butterflies try and enter their patch!

BRIMSTONE Probably my favourite butterfly, as it is such a herald of spring. These butterflies may emerge as early as February, having overwintered along with Peacocks, curly-winged Commas and Small Tortoiseshells. They are soon joined by other early fliers such as Orange Tips and Large Whites. Males are glorious yellow (females are off-white) and always rest with wings clasped together.

▲ *A perfect bamboo bee home.*

with bundled up chunks of bamboo (of a length that makes them lie flush with the mouth of the flowerpot or box) These pieces of bamboo should be cut so that their hollow interior is exposed. Solitary bees love places like this to make a home. Next you need to secure the bamboo in place, and fix the whole affair in a south facing sunny location, making sure no rainwater can drain inside the bamboo. Under the eaves of a shed is perfect.

BUTTERFLY BAR

It's an sign of the bad press moths get that you'll have far more luck convincing parents and friends that a butterfly bar is a good idea than a moth trap. To attract local butterflies, find a spot that receives warming sunlight, possibly close to a water source. Again, butterflies like sugary foods that are similar to nectar, and while they might not have the super-sense of moths, they can still trace heavy scents like rotting fruits from a good distance away. Try mashing up rotten bananas, plums – in fact any old soft fruit really. Some sugary water in a saucer will also work wonders. It's a good idea to create bright fake flowers, with the sugary reward at the centre. It is amazing how strongly bees and butterflies are attracted to bright colours – I've even had dopey bees trying to pollinate the bright red helmet I sometimes use when rock climbing!

▶ *Crickets and grasshoppers shed their skin a number of times throughout their lives. Keep your eyes peeled and you might see one emerging.*

Mountain biking

The idea of creating a hybrid between the BMX, road bike and racing bike is about 30 years old – a bike which would be able to conquer all kinds of terrain, have you purring through wild environments without the need for footslogging or the dreaded petrol engine. Since then, mountain biking has become incredibly popular, and brought with it numerous issues. Too many mountain bikes can cause terrible erosion (though nothing compared to a motorized trailbike) and some single track trails in the summer can bring walkers, dogs and cyclists into dangerous contact. All I can tell you is to make sure when you look at a map you are cycling on bridleways not footpaths, check access agreements in our national parks, and if you find yourself sharing a path with horses or walkers and dogs, SLOW DOWN!

That said, the mountain bike is a wondrous tool, and once you are fit and skilled enough it'll take you just about anywhere, which is perfect for the wildlife explorer. As I write this, my fingers are still a little stiff from frostnip after cycling (well, mostly carrying) my bike up the highest mountain in southern Britain... in a foot and a half of snow! Cronking Ravens filled the skies around me, and tracks of Foxes and Brown Hares peppered the glistening diamond dust snow. Wonderful. And the downhill was like sledging... except every time my bike hit a snowdrift I went flying over the handlebars!

Some of the nation's best mountain biking circuits are located in forests: Coed Y Brenin and Afan Forest in Wales; Leanachan and Wharncliffe in Scotland; Aston Hill and Swinley Forest in England. And that's just a small selection.

There's a lot to choose from with mountain bikes, and it's one of those sports that can become a bit of a money pit if you get too into it. My suggestion would be to keep it really simple until you've figured out if it's the sport for you, and have a good idea yourself of what your needs are.

FULL SUSPENSION VERSUS HARDTAIL

It's the old argument in mountain biking, and for me there's just no contest. A full suspension bike may be essential if you're just going to be haring down the near vertical single track off Ben Nevis, or doing lots of tricks and jumps. However, the extra bounce in the rear suspension wastes enormous amounts of your pedalling power when cycling uphill, on roads… well, anything other than downhill essentially. Also, having done several big ascents in the Alps, when the bike has had to go over my shoulder and be carried all day, I can tell you the heavier and clumsier full suspension bikes are a nightmare. If you're looking to explore just about anything the UK has to offer, a hardtail (a bike that only has suspension on the front forks and has the tail end fixed) or even a bike with no suspension at all is best. More important is to spend money on having a bike that is as light as possible, with good brakes (obviously!) and gears.

Navigating whilst on your bike is tricky. If I've got serious 'nav' to do, I mount a clipboard over the handlebars and clip a map (in a waterproof case) into it. Obviously, don't be tempted to read this whilst going 40 mph down a single-track hill! Handlebar-mounted GPS systems are getting cheaper and better all the time – but that's way too flashy for me!

▲ The Peak District National Park, seen here, is just one of many great spots to visit by bike.

BE PREPARED

When you're roadbiking, you're likely to be within sight of civilization, but offroad you could break down in a very isolated spot. Therefore every mountain biker should be able to mend a puncture, straighten a mildly buckled wheel, relink a broken chain and do minor repairs and adjustments to brakes and gears. I never go out on my bike without a tool kit that contains a spare inner tube and puncture repair kit, tyre irons, a pump, an all-in-one tool with chain link remover and Allen keys, and an adjustable wrench or pliers. Sounds like a lot, but I carry it all in the world's smallest backpack along with my bits, some fluids, a little cash, some choccie and my mobile phone.

Building a shelter

Here in the relatively modest forests of the UK, you'd have to be very unlucky, very foolish or both to get yourself into such a problematic situation that you have to fall back on basic survival techniques, but it can happen. If your adventuring takes you abroad to wilder woodlands, the chances of getting caught out and having to fend for yourself become higher. Though there are some sections in this book on finding wild food, the truth is that in a real survival situation that isn't your top priority – you can survive for weeks without food. You can even live a few days without water, but the effects of cold, wet and exposure can kill a person very quickly indeed. Your ability to make a shelter quickly could save your life. And I'm not talking about building a Swiss Family Robinson treetop castle complete with rope bridges and waterwheels – in fact, the most effective shelters are little bigger than you are, capable of providing maximum insulation and protection from the elements. At its simplest, this may just be rolling up in piles of dry leaves, or finding shelter in a cave or under a densely canopied tree.

Don't go around making shelters out of living vegetation just for fun. You may damage the woodland environment, and in England and Wales camping of any form is illegal in non-designated campsites unless you have the landowner's permission, so this is only for the direst emergency situations. If you do want to go hands-on you can gain practical experience of shelter-building on outdoor survival courses.

A-FRAME

The most basic of constructed shelters is an A-frame, made from a single long branch as a ridgeline, propped up at one or both ends by an A shape of two long branches. The walls of the shelter are made by lying branches side to side along this ridgeline. Next, you need to fill in the gaps, and cover as much as physically possible with whatever you can lay your hands on – ferns, leaves, mud, turf – anything! Always use more than you think you might need, and try and save the best dry material to keep you insulated from the ground inside – you lose more heat to the ground than you will to the air.

A modification of this can be done over a depression or ditch in the earth (although obviously not one that drains water!). Lay boughs across the top of the depression, and then the insulating materials.

TARPAULIN

The next level of shelter requires a tarp or other piece of material, which you may not have when in a survival situation. Such shelters do, however, provide much better protection against rain and wind, and are quicker and easier to construct. Create a ridgeline between two trees, using either a piece of string or a branch wedged or tied between the trees. The tarp is flopped over the ridgeline like a tent, then weighted down at the edges with rocks. When using tarps, don't be tempted to poke a hole in the tarp to tie off guy lines. Instead, pull in a fistful of tarp and tie off above it, or put a small pebble into the corner of the tarp, wrap it up and then tie off the other side with a loop of string.

▲ The simple A-frame construction of a basic shelter. You're not likely to need to build your own shelter in the UK, but anything can happen! Don't cut down trees or shrubs just for fun; if you're interested in learning how to build your own shelter, try an outdoor survival course.

HAMMOCK

The next level up is creating a hammock such as that shown in the photo. To be honest, you're going to need to have brought almost everything for this particular shelter with you, but it has the advantage of keeping you off the ground and away from the bugs that potentially live there. These shelters can be really cold at night though, as you have no insulating layer beneath you. Choose two trees that are approximately 4 m apart, and ensure there are no nasty spiky roots or branches beneath you that could impale you if your shelter was to collapse.

Five forest finds

RED SQUIRREL Our native squirrel has come under extraordinary pressure over the last years from the destruction of its habitat, the deadly parapox virus, and the invasive American Grey Squirrel. It's pretty sad to see the red squeezed out to northern England, Wales and Scotland – we had Red Squirrels on the small farm I grew up on in Surrey, but now the area has none at all. There are probably 140,000 Reds and 5 million Greys in Britain today. The Greys were introduced over 100 years ago for reasons that totally escape me; it seems to have been purely for the amusement of the Victorians. Whatever you think about the Grey versus Red argument is pretty much irrelevant, as the Grey is clearly a born survivor and here to stay. However, our own native Red is a prettier creature, with a softer, less ratty face, beautiful colours, cute tufty ears and more dainty manners. These days, Red Squirrels in the UK are mainly found in conifer forests (though they lived in all kinds of woodland before the arrival of the Greys) where they feed mostly on

pine cones. They build an untidy drey, in which a litter of (usually two or three) kits will be born in the spring, with potentially a second litter later in the summer.

BLACKCAP These dapper birds are mostly summer visitors to our shores, though some may occur in winter, and are most often found in woodlands, where their magnificent song can be heard piercing the gloom on the forest floor. They are greyish warblers – males are easily recognized by the black cap (though to confuse matters females' caps are chestnut-brown). The fluty song has similarities to the Blackbird's, but some think it so spectacular as to nickname the Blackcap the 'Northern Nightingale'!

STOAT

Though Stoats can be almost the same length as Weasels, they can also weigh nine times more! In both species the male is bigger than the female. The tip of the Stoat's tail is always black, which is the best ID feature. The Stoat is one of the world's greatest predators. While a Weasel will rarely take anything bigger than a vole, Stoats can take fully grown rabbits, which could be four times their body weight. Both Stoats and Weasels are hated by gamekeepers, as they may take gamebirds, as well as their eggs and chicks. If you're in the wild woodlands of Scottish Highlands, there is a small chance of encountering the closely related Pine Marten, which has a yellow bib, a long bushy tail, and is a good deal larger than even the biggest Stoat.

ROE DEER This is one of our two native species of deer (the Red Deer being the other), but the Roe Deer we see today are mostly descended from immigrants. They were hunted almost to extinction during the 1700s, but after an extensive

reintroduction programme in the 1800s are back in force. These are really pretty little deer, with a white patch on the rump, a black 'moustache' and a narrower face and more upright ears than the Red Deer. They are often solitary, and are quite nervous animals with great hearing and sense of smell. When alarmed, Roe Deer may let out a distinctive bark to warn nearby animals.

WOOD MOUSE One of the commonest British mammals; if you put out some nuts or jam in woodland, it's pretty much guaranteed a Wood Mouse will appear.

If you can't do with sitting up all night to get a sighting, put a little flour on the ground around your bait – the mice should leave perfect tracks for you to identify in the morning. Wood Mice don't hibernate, but make nests for the winter, each of which may accommodate as many as five mice. They have larger ears and eyes than the House Mouse, and a more appealing general demeanour.

Woodland tracks and signs

Obviously, when you're tracking, the first thing to do is to take a good look around you at the surroundings; open ground will yield rabbits and perhaps Brown Hares, denser tree cover and there's bound to be a squirrel or two around. Some of the most common prints to be seen are obviously made by domestic animals, so get used to sussing out what those look like in order to remove them from the equation (for example, a Fox print is generally smaller and much more compact than a dog print). Other signs can tell you very interesting things about the wildlife in your area.

WILD BOAR

The Wild Boar roamed Britain's forest from the last ice age, right up until it was hunted out about 300 years ago. However, escapees from boar farms – and perhaps a few intentional releases – have resulted in Wild Boars being well and truly back in certain forests around the UK. I can't reveal any sites, as their presence is quite a controversial subject, and some people would rather they weren't around, but they are easier to track than to see. The Wild Boar is best tracked at its wallow site, which will be a shallow pool of much disturbed mud, used by the boar to detach parasites from its skin. The hoof print is cloven, similar to a deer print, but with a pair of prominent dewclaw prints behind the two hoof halves (dewclaws are extra claws on the inside of the leg). You may find scratching posts on trees, and huge areas of ground that have been so heavily rooted up that they look as if a JCB has been at work there.

MUNTJAC DEER

These small deer are most active at dawn and dusk, and may spend most of the day hidden away in long grass or thickets. You may find the impressions of their small bodies (no larger than a labrador) pressed into the grass. The droppings are small and rabbit-like and easily break into pellets, the hoof (with no evident dewclaw) provides the smallest cloven print found in the UK, and can often be found on quite well-travelled paths; though they'd certainly never walk that way while humans are around!

SONG THRUSH

If you're wandering through a woodland and suddenly come across a pile of smashed-up snail shells you've discovered the work of the blacksmith of the woods, the Song Thrush. It uses an anvil, usually a solid chunk of stone, to break snail shells. Research suggests Song Thrushes only feed this way when the ground is too hard to dig up worms. To tell Mistle and Song Thrushes apart, I remember M for Mistle and Medium-sized (with its head seeming too small for its body) and S for Song and Small (and perfectly proportioned).

▲ This collection of broken snail shells is the work of a Song Thrush.

TAWNY OWL

The most interesting signs left by our native owls are their pellets. Owl pellets resemble good-sized fox droppings, but are neatly rounded at both ends rather than tapered and pointed at one end. They are regurgitated from the mouth, and contain all the bits of prey that the owl can't digest properly. Usually the Tawny Owl will devour its prey in one gulp; and the vast majority of the time it's an unlucky vole. Tease the pellet apart with a little water and a paintbrush, and you will find fur, teeth, some bones – perhaps even a tiny skull or two!

SHREW

These tiny mammals are among the busiest little predators around, and rarely stop filling their faces with insect food. In spots much used by shrews you may find piles of discarded inedible insect bits. The track shows five slender toes on each foot, and the scat is made of small pellets with tapered ends, and again, perhaps bits of insect that have no nutriment such as wing casings.

SQUIRREL, MOUSE, RAT ... OR DORMOUSE?

The Hazel is a small tree, rarely reaching 10 m, but it is really important as a food source when its nuts ripen in the autumn – they're rich in both fats and protein, and yummy too. The most obvious hazelnut munchers are squirrels, but they're not the only beasts in the woods who like nuts. Examining the husks of the nut will let you know who's been feeding.

Is the husk split down the middle? Then it's the work of a clumsy but powerful Grey Squirrel; they take the nuts in their front paws and wreak havoc with their powerful rodent incisors. Is the husk gnawed with messy scratch marks, with a hole where the kernel can be extracted? This is the work of a Wood Mouse, or possibly a Brown Rat – not hazel specialists, but still impressive tooth skills! Or does the husk have a perfect hole that looks almost as if it's been done by a machine, no messy scratches? Then you're lucky enough to be in the presence of the hazelnut specialist: the Hazel Dormouse. This adorable little critter is probably asleep in the tree high above you right now!

▶ *These hazelnuts have without doubt been munched by the hazel specialist: the dormouse.*

Ultimate critter cribs

As natural woodland habitats are hacked down to make way for human housing, animal real estate is becoming more and more valuable. A great way to help out the wildlife in your area is to make homes they can take up residence in. Although all of the following will probably be more likely to work in your local woodland, with a bit of careful planning you can put any of these animal homes in a decent-sized garden, which will have the added advantage of attracting animals into your world.

BAT BOX

Though some people have weird phobias about bats, the truth is that our most common bats are absolutely tiny (Pipistrelles weigh as little as a 50p piece!), extremely cute and munch down flying insects in incredible numbers. Add to that the fact that some species are among the most threatened mammals in the UK, and making them a home seems like a great idea. Bats need summer daytime roosts, breeding sites and winter hibernation sites. Boxes can be bought cheaply from good garden centres, but making your own is pretty easy. Just create a wooden box with a sloping roof so the rain runs off. It should be no bigger than a shoe box, and half that size would work fine, and have an entrance slot (rather than a hole) no more than 2 cm wide. Make sure the wood is untreated raw timber, as preservatives can kill bats. Place bat boxes in groups around trees, or perhaps under the eaves of buildings and high enough up that

▲ You can buy ready-made bat boxes, or make your own.

they are safe from cats; if you can get them 5 m off the ground that'd be ideal. Once your box is in place do not disturb it, unless you are 100 per cent certain it is unoccupied. All British bats are protected, and it is illegal to interfere with them in any way.

OWL BOX

This is definitely one that will work much better in woodlands than in your back garden – very few people are lucky enough to have owls nesting so close to them. However, it's got to be worth a try. Each different species of owl has a design of owl box that is most likely to attract them – Little Owl boxes are like bobbins, while Barn Owl boxes are often shaped like weird pyramids. Again, these are all available quite reasonably from eco-goods suppliers or garden centres, but it's quite easy to make your own. The Tawny Owl is your best bet to try and attract, as it is the most common of our owls, and though it would ideally choose to make its home in woodland or farmland, it is often found nesting in city parks and even gardens. Boxes are tube-like, to mimic the tree holes the owls would naturally choose, with

a letterbox-shaped opening, and a perch outside the box for them to land on. The box should be located as high up on trees as possible, and should be south-facing in order to avoid wind, unless you live somewhere with prevailing wind that predictably comes from another direction.

▲ *With lots of luck and the right box, you might be able to entice an owl to move in close by.*

HEDGEHOG HOME

Everybody wants snuffling Hedgehogs in their garden – apart from Tiggywinkles being utterly adorable, they are great natural pest control, munching their way through hundreds of slugs and snails that would otherwise chomp people's vegetable patches to bits. When filming with a rescue centre in Scotland that specialized in rehousing rehabilitated Hedgehogs, we found they had years-long waiting lists for people dying to have Hedgehogs introduced to their gardens. Hedgehog homes need to be sturdy boxes made of thick wood, which can keep out dogs and badgers. Most commercially available hedgehog homes will have an extended or offset doorway, which will make

▲ *Build a Hedgehog a home and you'll be providing a resting place and a safe spot to spend the winter.*

it more difficult for predators to stick their nose in. These homes have two functions; firstly as a nest for Hedgehogs when they are up and about, but also as a 'hibernaculum' during the winter months when they'll be fast asleep. Though they will bring in their own bedding, it doesn't hurt to help them out by putting in a bit of dry straw. On this topic, be very careful before burning piles of leaves or strimming wild corners of your garden. Untold numbers of Hedgehogs and other animals meet a grisly end this way every year.

BUG PALACES

For me, the joy of having loads of different cool creepy-crawlies about is worthwhile in itself. However, even for those who don't really like bugs, there are great advantages to having a good crop of them in your garden. Bats and birds will be much more likely to frequent an area that's full of bugs, and simple bug homes will also be used by our native reptiles and amphibians as a place to lay low for the winter. The simplest and most effective home is just a log pile; a whole bunch of old rotting chunks of wood. If you live in the south-east, Stag Beetles may lay their eggs in your wood pile, and their grotesque grubs will live for years munching away inside. Inevitable woodlice, centipedes and millipedes will soon take up residence, whilst newts, frogs, toads, Slow-worms and even snakes may lay up there during the winter freeze.

Another great way to ensure a garden full of the most exciting bugs is to choose the right 'nectar rich' garden plants. In the spring big butterfly attracters are Honesty, Primrose, Sweet Violet and Wallflowers; in the summer Buddleia, Lavender, Marjoram, Red Valerian and night-scented stock. In the autumn Sweet Scabious, Blackthorn and Helenium are good nectar providers. For attracting other insects such as bees, you may want to consider plants like Columbine, Yellow Loosestrife, Honeysuckle and Ragged Robin. A patch of garden that is left wild, with brambles and nettles abundant, is also a wonderful way of ensuring wildlife has a place to hide, and caterpillars have food plants to munch on. A slab of corrugated iron left on the ground will soon have hundreds of critters hiding beneath it – if you're lucky they might include one of our native reptiles such as the Grass Snake. It is vital to make sure that once you've set up a log pile you don't disturb it as this will definitely kill something; maybe just a few common bugs, but possibly something really special.

BIRD BOXES

Trying to provide homes for the many species of birds that can choose to live in our woods and gardens would be a huge undertaking. Every one has different needs when they make a nest – having their own niche enables them to live side by side without too many problems. It's a subject for another whole book really, so I'll just give you a few basics. Have a hinged side or top to the box so you can clean it out (in the autumn, when any chicks have long since fledged). Make sure there are drainage holes in the bottom of the box in case your roof doesn't do its job, and make sure the floor of the box is set up inside the walls. Not many birds use perches on the outside of boxes; Sparrows and Starlings are exceptions. It's an idea to remove perches from boxes you buy, as they can offer a helping hand to predators that may want to get inside. Keep bird boxes well spaced out to avoid conflicts, and keep them well clear of places cats can reach. In fact, if you have cats maybe forget bird boxes altogether – even if the cat can't get to the birds or their chicks, there's evidence that adult birds spend so much time stressing about the presence of cats that their success in raising chicks is massively reduced. Use wood for your bird box, not metal or plastics, as these can overheat.

Orchids alive

Perhaps no plants on the planet have inspired as much obsession and insanity as the orchids. Collectors have killed and died to get hold of certain exotic species; some have been collected to extinction while others are quite literally worth more than their weight in gold. Our very own Lady's Slipper orchid is a great example; collected in such numbers by horticulturists that by the beginning of the 19th century it was believed extinct. However, in one secret site in Yorkshire a single plant survived; I've actually met one of the women whose full-time job it was to camp out next to the orchid and protect it from thieves. There are about 50 species of orchids here in the UK, most of which are small and exquisite. Some of the best places to go looking are marshy meadows, the edges of woodlands, and even overgrown roadside verges. However, when you find an orchid, don't be tempted to pick – draw, paint or photograph your prize, but leave it where it is.

▶ Bee Orchid. Larger and showier than the Fly Orchid, this species is also more common and widespread, although not found in the north of Scotland. After the Bee Orchid has flowered once, it generally dies. It likes chalky or sandy soils, and can even be found on overgrown sand-dunes, loving open sunny aspects.

Four fantastic orchids

FLY ORCHID

AUTUMN LADY'S TRESSES

You could easily overlook this small orchid; the flower is often no larger than my thumbnail. However, when you get up close, it really is a work of art. The delicate arrangement of its petals imitates a fly, enticing amorous insects, which then pollinate the flower. The wire-like upper petals look like antenna, two bright patches beneath resemble eyes, and the metallic sheen is much like that of a fly's body catching the light. The eye patches are actually blobs of pollen, which stick onto the heads of visiting insects and are then carried off to other flowers. Fly Orchids can be found at the edge of woodlands and in recently cleared land, mostly in southern England.

As with so many of our orchids, this flower is thought to be in decline because of the loss of suitable places for it to grow. However, it has shown itself to be pretty tough, and can make a good recovery once grasslands are left fallow for a while. It's small, and ever such a pretty plant, getting its name from the similarity of its bloom to a spiralling ringlet of a lady's hair. Each flower is very small, shaped like a tube, and pollinated by aphids. The stem is leafless, and when it's not flowering, all there is to see is a small rosette of leaves on the ground; this dies away before the flower emerges.

PYRAMIDAL ORCHID

LIZARD ORCHID

In comparison to the other orchids mentioned here, this is quite a common flower, found brightening up summer meadows throughout the south and east of England. The flowers are a delightful pinkish purple colour, and unmistakable, as they're formed into a tight pyramid. Pollinated by butterflies and day-flying moths, the colourful flower is often adorned with an even more colourful insect. The butterfly or moth inserts its proboscis into the flower to get a nip of sweet nectar, and in the process it gets pasted with pollen to pass on to the next flower it lands on.

Yet another orchid with a weird resemblance to another living organism, though in this case (and that of the even weirder Man and Monkey Orchids) it's obviously not a mimic attempting to attract a potential pollinator! Well, unless lizards and very small men and monkeys have taken to fluttering round flowers... Even more strange is that this orchid is said to smell like wet goat! Unfortunately one of the best places to go looking for this flower is on motorway verges – more and more wildlife is finding respite in these environments, and of course it's way too dangerous and noisy to go looking for flowers at the side of the M1!

Wild foods: a fungal feast

Fungi thrive in damp conditions, and in late summer through to early winter our woods are full of some of the world's most delicious free foods. Truffles, for example are possibly the most valuable of natural foods – though your chances of finding their underground location without a specially trained dog or pig are very slim. The produce of many woodlands is protected, and you should enquire of the owners before collecting fungi for the pot. Even more importantly, there are several fungi in Britain that are potentially deadly. It is a wise move to learn these before the potentially edible species, so as to avoid any mix-ups. The best way to learn is to go out with an expert, perhaps on an organized 'fungus foray'. Good field guides exist but there's no substitute for expert knowledge out in the field. Never eat raw wild fungi, and if in doubt; just DON'T EAT IT!

CHANTERELLE

Among the most prized of all our native fungi, with a pale yellow flesh, and a vague smell of apricots. It is funnel-shaped without downturned cap edges, and the gills run down the stem. The False Chanterelle (which could make you sick) is usually orange with more tightly packed gills that stop at the stem, and often has downturned cap edges. Clean Chanterelles thoroughly, and cook them straight away as they don't keep well, and for at least fifteen minutes as otherwise they can be a bit tough.

CEP

Members of the genus *Boletus* are recognized by having spongy, porous material under the cap, no gills, and a smell described as being like dough. Our best loved is known as the 'penny bun' or Cep. Investigate older mushrooms carefully as they are prone to maggots, and you may have to discard the stems. This has a nutty flavour and is one of the most prized by chefs.

WOOD MUSHROOM

An absolutely delicious mushroom found in all kinds of woodlands, late autumn into early winter, and probably the nearest thing to the large mushrooms you'll find in your local supermarket. The cap is smooth and white, the gills pinkish.

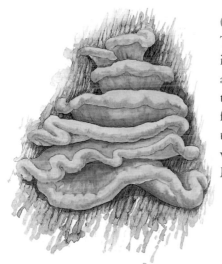

CHICKEN OF THE WOODS

This is relatively easy to safely identify and collect; it's a bright yellow bracket fungus with no gills and a soft texture. Cut off chunks near to the tree rather than just ripping them off (this could kill the parent fungus). The remarkable thing about this fungus is that it lives up to its name! When cooked it behaves very much like chicken, with flaky white meat. Make sure it is very well cooked though.

AND TWO TO STAY AWAY FROM!

DEATH CAP

This is the species you *must* know before trying to collect wild fungus, as it does not look particularly nasty, but can destroy your liver and eventually kill you, one mushroom containing enough toxin to kill three people. Frequently found beneath oak trees, it has a white stalk and gills, a yellow, greenish or grey cap (although a pure white form exists too), and a sack-like, bulbous lump at the base of the stalk.

FLY AGARIC

With its red, white-spotted cap, this large poisonous mushroom is familiar and easily recognized. Symptoms of poisoning begin within a couple of hours and include nausea, vomiting, diarrhoea, excessive salivation, sweating, watering eyes, difficulty breathing, dilated pupils, excitability and confusion. Although very unpleasant, Fly Agaric poisoning is rarely serious and recovery usually occurs within 12 hours.

Wild cooking

Knowing how to make a fire in a variety of different situations is one of the most important skills an adventurer can have. (It's covered in more detail in the Freshwater chapter.) Be extremely careful whenever you make a fire, and only do so in the countryside when you have no choice. Without the landowner's permission it's illegal, and the risk of starting a forest fire is too significant to ignore – uncontrolled fires can devastate habitats and wildlife, and land you in a big heap of trouble. If you want to cook over a fire, do it in your garden or at a campsite that allows fires – and remain extremely vigilant at all times.

▲ *A green stick cooker like this can easily be knocked up in a few minutes.*

Once you have a fire up and running, there are various ways to cook over it. One of the best methods is the tepee cooker shown here. Freshly cut green sticks will smoulder, but not burn, particularly if kept a reasonable distance from the flames or embers. To make a tepee cooker, you'll need to make a tent-like structure from three or four stout sticks embedded into the ground, then brought together and bound at their apex. Next, depending on how hot the flames are, how high they are jumping, and how long you want to cook your food for, you need to create a platform for meat, fish or vegetables to rest on. About a foot off the ground is usually pretty good. Bind a stick parallel to the ground between each of the stout outer sticks. Then you can lay a griddle of other green sticks across these. In this photo all of the binding was done with pieces of vine, but string obviously works just as well.

A less sturdy but simpler arrangement is just to find a bunch of large boulders and lay them to either side of the fire. Then you can balance your green stick griddle across the flames on the top of the rocks.

Both of these methods also work really well for smoking meats and fish. This makes the food last longer and renders it resistant to infestations by mould and maggots. In order to do this, you'll need to follow all the steps above, but when the fire is good and strong, add a pile of green deciduous leaves to it. You will need to seal in the smoke by blocking off the corners of the tepee with turf or something similar, and leave for a day, ensuring the fire doesn't go out! Rubbing salt into the meat also helps the preserving process.

▶ *A woodland coppice alive with wild garlic. The bulbs and flowers are edible and the leaves are great raw in salads.*

Coast

The place where land meets sea is one of the most challenging of all landscapes for life, but it is also one of the most exciting for a naturalist. From beachcombing in the intertidal zone to freediving round a rocky inlet, the end of the land is the perfect place for the adventure naturalist to explore.

Make the most of the coast

Twice a day dry land is soaked with salt water, and these rhythms drive everything at the water's edge, from the flocks of wading birds following the bounty of intertidal mud to the crabs that scavenge the still waters of temporary rockpools. The different zones of the seashore all have their own unique fauna, and a variety of exciting ways to make the most of them. As a youngster, going to the seaside was always the highlight of the holidays. My sister and I would spend days poking through Cornish rockpools discovering endless unusual creatures, body-surfing in Atlantic breakers or sat on the pier with a crab line, praying for a huge piecrust-shelled crab to take the bait. (Admittedly, I also spent a lot of time shivering blue with cold behind my grandma's windbreak, with sea salt burns where my legs rubbed against my saggy trunks, and hands so wrinkled from the sea they looked as though they'd been pickled in vinegar.) These days, I still get the same joy out of coaxing a Butterfish from under an anemone-encrusted rock, or pulling in a good crab, but I am drawn more and more to explore the shoreline beyond the reach of the holidaying crowd. To find that foreign land, all you need is time, experience and a little adventurous spirit.

There are many ways to make the most of the coast, and they're always fun in themselves even if you never actually see any wildlife. Surfing is not an activity you would undertake in order to watch wildlife, although I've had dolphins and seals leaping over my board whilst sat out beyond the breakers waiting for a wave, and just about every surfer on the planet believes that surfing puts them 'in tune' with the sea. Sea kayaking, coasteering, beachcombing and rockpooling, however, are some of the most reliable and most rewarding ways of finding unusual animals and plants in elemental landscapes.

The tides drive life at the water's edge, and when you're exploring the coastal environment, the tides will be all-important to you too. What time of day will bring the heaviest surf? When is it going to be possible to get your sea kayak out through the breakers, and when are you going to be able to go hunting for lugworms without risking the terror of the turning tide?

While it's perhaps the untamed wild beauty of the seashore that draws us in, the unpredictable nature of the coasts can make this one of the most dangerous places for a naturalist to be. On a filming trip in Alaska, my team was so engrossed with filming Grizzly Bears fishing in a river near the sea that we totally overlooked the incoming tide, and were cut off in a near-inescapable rock amphitheatre by waters that seemed to come up within minutes. All of a sudden, from being completely in control of the situation, we found ourselves trapped with two fully grown and very hungry horse-sized Grizzlies eyeing us suspiciously. The escape was neither pretty or dignified; we got a good soaking, my camera ended up on the bottom of the river and the rest of our kit floated out to sea, but if the bears hadn't had quite so much salmon to feed on, it might have been an awful lot worse.

The deaths of 21 cockle fishermen on the tidal sands of Morecambe in 2004 further illustrate the severity of the danger created by the tides. *Always* check and be aware of the tides if you're spending time at the coast.

Rockpooling

Rockpools are areas of standing water which have become trapped in rocks near the water's edge as the sea retreats with the tide. The rockpools found further up the beach lose much of their fresh water to evaporation and so can become punishingly saline. Those that have the greatest variety of life are found closer to the sea, where conditions are more constant. If you lumber up to a rockpool noisily in the middle of the day, it will appear to be almost empty of life because everything will be hiding away. In order to get the animals out in the open, you need to drop your body down below the skyline so you are not so visible, keep quiet, and then give the wildlife a good reason for coming out to investigate... bait!

One way to coax out shoreside creatures is to take a very small amount potted fish paste or some ham or bacon from your sandwiches and toss a little of that into an open part of the rockpool. During the daytime few of the gems of the pool will be in plain view, but patience pays dividends. Leave a nice bit of tasty bait in the open, and soon something is bound to come and investigate. It may just be a few dainty prawns, and then the odd blenny or rock goby, but in bigger deeper pools you may even catch more spectacular species of the deeper sea stranded by the tides. As a kid, I could literally spend hours picking my way through rockpools for peculiar wildlife.

Examine the pools from the sides, move carefully and slowly and if you move any stones in the rockpool replace them exactly where they were after you've had a look underneath. Don't pull any creatures off the rocks, and if you net any free-moving animals for a closer look, do so with great care, keep the net submerged, and let them go as soon as you've finished. Using a small pocket mirror tied to a stick is a less intrusive way to help you to peek sneakily under crevices and ledges to see what's lurking beneath. Perhaps try fixing one to the stick end of your scoop net.

To get a fish-eye view on what's occurring underwater, a swimming mask pushed gingerly into the surface of the water will give you a window into this weird world. Rockpools at night are also fascinating; much of the life that hides during the day will be out in full force in the dark. Your torchlight will bring to life the magnificent colours of sea squirts, anemones and starfish – perhaps even nudibranchs or chitons. Obviously, all the warnings about coastal dangers are even more important in the dark.

▶ Take some time to investigate rockpools and you'll discover a fascinating world of wildlife, especially if you entice the creatures out with a little bait. Keep quiet and still and you might even see something really unusual. Britain has thousands of miles of coastline, so we're spoilt for choice when it comes to locations. Particularly good sites for rockpooling can be found around Devon and in the north of Scotland.

Rockin' rockpool residents

STAR ASCIDIAN These beautiful animals are sessile (they don't move) and live in star-shaped colonies of up to 12 individuals with a central breathing hole. They can be found in rockpools, but are more often seen encrusting stones on the lower shore. The larva resembles a tadpole with a hollow nerve chord, so biologists place this species in the phylum Chordata – more closely related to fish, and even to us, than to sponges or corals.

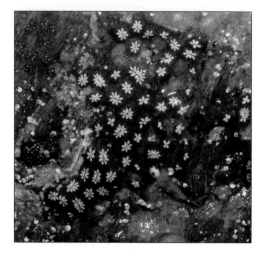

SNAKELOCKS ANEMONE The sticky purple-tipped tentacles of this anemone hang in the water column to entrap items of food that float by. The green colour of the medusa-like tentacles comes from photosynthetic algae in its cells. Unlike other species of anemone the Snakelocks cannot withdraw its tentacles so is more often found in the safety of deep pools. You might also find Beadlet and Strawberry Anenomes, which look like little molten Jelly Tots.

BUTTERFISH One of the triumphs of the rockpool, adult Butterfish can reach 20 cm long. Trying to catch one is like trying to catch a fish that's been smeared in butter – not easy! They're easy to tell apart from the closely related blennies and gobies by their length and the much smaller head, and are great parents, with both mum and dad taking turns at minding the eggs.

SHORE CLINGFISH or **CORNISH SUCKER**
A really pretty and odd little fish, which
appears to have two bright blue eyes
ringed in red on its back. These are just
flashy colourings, and its actual eyes are
on the sides of its head where they
should be. If you pick one up, it will cling
to your hand with a sucker on its
underside, which feels decidedly peculiar.

HAIRY PORCELAIN CRAB Let's face it; if
you find a crab round the shores of
Britain, it's going to be... a Common Shore
Crab. Is it green or brown, with a sort of
serrated edge to the shell? If so then it's
almost certainly the
Common Shore. However, we
do have lots of other
species, some of which are
absolutely dazzling. The Hairy
Porcelain Crab is most often
found under a stone near the low tide
mark, and is so small and well
camouflaged you may well miss it
completely. If you find what appears to be
an empty complete crab shell, this is
what's left behind when a crab grows and
sheds its old skin.

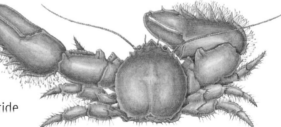

Terrific tides

Tides are the regular rising and falling of the earth's large bodies of water. All of the surfaces of the Earth are pulled by gravity towards the Moon and the sun, just like two magnets attract each other. The solid surfaces of the Earth are massive enough to resist, but as the seas and oceans are liquid, they are greatly influenced by this attraction, as well as by the centrifugal force exerted as the earth spins. Being 400 times closer to us than the sun, the Moon has a greater effect on tides. As the Moon rotates around the Earth, gravitational force pulls on the side of the Earth closest to the Moon, causing the seas to bulge. On the other side of the world there is an equivalent bulge These are the high tides which happen twice a day.

When the moon is full or new, the gravitational pull of the Moon and Sun are combined, which results in extra high and extra low tides – these

▲ One of Britain's great natural spectacles, the Severn Bore offers hardy surfers a very long ride indeed.

are known as spring tides (nothing to do with the season). During quarter phases of the Moon, the Sun and Moon are at right angles and cancel each other's affects out somewhat, resulting in smaller, or neap tides.

Tides vary greatly around the world, and are much less noticeable at the equator, while the highest tides are in the north – most famously in Canada at the Bay of Fundy in Nova Scotia, where tides can rise and fall 20 m. Other examples of great natural events caused by the tides include the famous tidal bore of our own River Severn. At certain times of year, especially large tides cause a metre-high wave of water to sloosh as much as 14 miles upriver. I tried to surf the Severn bore in a Canadian canoe some years back, and found out quite how unpredictable it could be. The night before, I was camping on the riverbank and the bore raged past, powering up the bank and carrying my boat and nearly my tent off upriver; wading around in the dark in February freezing water trying to save my possessions was not one of my adventure highlights. The next day, when we were supposed to be filming the wave and the cameras were rolling... well, I've seen bigger ripples in ice cream!

The secret to surviving an encounter with the tides is a good tidal table and the knowledge of how to read it properly.

Wading birds

Our wading birds live their lives by the turning of the tides, and the various species have a number of different strategies for getting the most out of the bounty buried like treasure in the sands.

PROBERS

Curlews are archetypal probers, sinking their long, curved bills into sand and intertidal mud to try and locate crustaceans, worms and molluscs deep beneath the surface. They have the longest bills of any of our wading birds (as much as nine inches long). From April to July they head for breeding habitat, often in inland, upland areas; thereafter they head to the coast to feed. That gigantic bill means they are the only birds that stand a chance of digging down to get lugworms – choice bits of chow that tend to burrow down very deep into the mud.

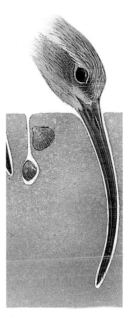

▲ Curlew

The vibrating call Curlews make on the wing is one of my favourite sounds, although it is probably topped by the weird 'out of tune radio' of the Lapwing!

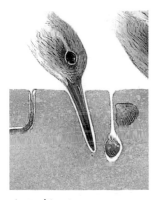

▲ Redshank

The Dunlin, Sanderling and Knot are probers too. Gathering together in tightly packed groups, they can often be seen in fast-moving, low-flying flocks that seem to function as a single organism. In particular, winter-flying Knot flocks are among the most spectacular coastal sights imaginable. None of these birds have bills long enough to get down to ragworms or lugworms, and instead they may dabble with molluscs such as the plentiful Laver Spire shell and cockles, which live near the surface, and the Peppery Furrow shell, which is found a little deeper. Crustaceans such as tiny mud shrimps can be found at densities of 11,000 animals in every square metre.

GLEANERS

Plovers are archetypal gleaners, with a much shorter bill and a stop-run-peck feeding method, quite similar to a Blackbird on a lawn. In order for this strategy to work, they need to be feeding in an area that is free from other birds that might frighten prey away.

▲ Grey Plover

Ringed Plovers are among the smaller shorebirds, and scurry along the beach feeding on invertebrates on the surface of the sand. Turnstones and Purple Sandpipers also have quite short bills and a similar feeding strategy. You're most likely to see them around rocks, turning them over to see if there's food hiding underneath.

Seashore tracks and signs

Soft, wet sand can be the perfect substrate for making clear prints that are easy to identify. At different times of year, you're likely to get a different ensemble of animals at the shore; pay attention to what's around before making bold guesses with your detective work.

DUCKS AND GEESE

The messy white, black and green slop that ducks and geese leave behind is quite distinctive, and where these birds are numerous, it's everywhere The print is also quite noticeable; the three forward facing toes have clear webbing between them, and the foot has a tendency to face inwards as the bird walks.

SHOREBIRDS

You can clearly tell these apart from the ducks, as they have four narrow toes (apart from Sanderlings, which have only three), though the rear one may not show. The print is very nearly symmetrical, quite neat, and claws may be clearly discerned. The scat is small and semi liquid.

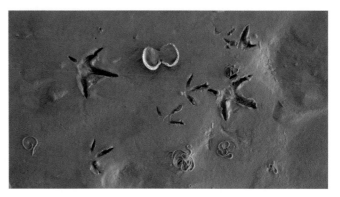

▲ *Shorebird prints are easy to spot on mud or sand.*

GULLS

The gulls can be pretty big in the UK – the Great Black-backed is the largest species in the world and is of quite intimidating proportions. By the way, take care not to call them 'seagulls' as birders tend to get quite upset about this; they're just gulls. The prints have three toes pointing forwards with webbing, and do not turn inwards as much as duck prints. The toes are also more divergent. The liquid scat is obvious to anyone who's every spent any time at the seaside.

FOX

First off, you need to set this print apart from a dog's print, and that's not easy. Put simply, the Fox print is more compact, and smaller than most breeds of dog. The claws are prominent, and the inside toe is larger than the outside. The scat, however, is very different from dog poo (though it is of great interest to most dogs, who love rolling in it). The scat has a tapered tail and it may contain hair, berries and insect parts. Luckily, the musty, pungent odour is nothing like as offensive as dog poo on your shoe if you don't notice it until it's too late!

OTTER

Otters have large, webbed feet (though the webbing may be difficult to see). The hind paws are very wide with five toes, and there may be some tail drag. Otter scat (and occasionally the scat of fellow mustelids – members of the weasel family) is known as spraint. It is used to mark territory, often dumped in latrines, and will contain oily fishy remains. It has a powerful scent that some have described as flowery or hay like. Otters are still quite rare in the UK, but the west coast of Scotland has a healthy population.

▲ *Otter spraint is tarry and slimy when fresh and has a long-lasting smell.*

Flotsam and jetsam

One of the sad side effects of our cruise-liner sea culture is the enormous amount of junk discarded into our seas, much of which will very soon find its way back to the shore. 'Mailboats' – small sealed wooden casks traditionally used to post letters by casting them into the sea – from the British archipelago of St Kilda have turned up over a year later on the shores of Scandinavia and even America.

Much flotsam and jetsam is ugly plastic nastiness (and you will be doing wildlife a great favour if you join a task force to clear rubbish from your local beach), but some real gems turn up on our shores. Wave-smoothed driftwood can produce some of the most startling natural art for those with a creative bent – my sister makes picture frames, sideboards and carvings from pieces she's found washed up on the beach.

The sandy shore

Though it may look like the beginnings of a desert, a stretch of dunes and sandy shoreline are actually places of plenty, and abound with life. I've watched Brown Hares boxing on Chesil Beach, and seen gulls fighting a Fox for food in the dunes of north Wales whilst chasing Natterjack Toads there. Lift any chunk of seaweed in the strandline and you'll be faced with hundreds of little Sandhoppers – little creatures that exist by recycling decomposing material at the water's edge – as well as what look like giant woodlice, but are actually called Sea Slaters.

Top finds at the sandy shore

COMMON SAND WASP This impressive insect is set apart by its tiny waist and long, slim, red-and-black abdomen, held upwards at an angle when the wasp is in flight. These wasps will paralyse a caterpillar many times larger than themselves using their potent stings. They then fly the unfortunate insect back to their burrow for their larvae to feed on.

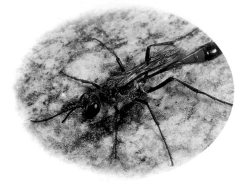

DUNE WOLF SPIDER These fearsome hunters spend a good deal of time in burrows in the sand, but also run around seeking prey from May to August. The females can often be seen carrying tiny white balls around with them – their silken egg sacks full of eggs which will eventually hatch into tiny spiderlings.

MERMAID'S PURSE A delightfully romantic name for an artefact that is evidence of some of our most spectacular sea beasties. Commonly seen around our shores, this is the egg case of some of our smaller sharks and rays, including the Lesser-spotted Dogfish and Undulate Ray, which lay their eggs not far from shore. The tendrils at the corners of the purse are used to attach these to seaweed until the young emerge, but often the purse comes adrift and is washed ashore. If the purse is broken open, the shark has probably hatched out successfully.

SAND LIZARD Is the male Sand Lizard Britain's most beautiful creature? I think so! Those vibrant green breeding colours make these little jewels one of our most eye-catching sights, best seen on warm days when they bask in the sun at the side of pathways. You're most likely to see one around the dunes and heathlands in the south of England, although they are also found near Merseyside and there is an introduced population on Scotland's Isle of Coll. The females are somewhat duller, but still very pretty little lizards.

Whilst the Common Lizard gives birth to live young, Sand Lizards lay eggs. Courtship follows a bout of wrestling between males; they grab each other in their jaws and roll around a bit until the stronger lizard emerges victorious. Their diet ranges from insects, slugs and spiders to flowers and fruit.

RAZOR SHELL The name comes from the resemblance they bear to an old-fashioned straight razor. The main body of this bivalve mollusc is held within the two halves of the shell, which buries down deep into the sand near the low tide mark. You may occasionally see the feeding siphon sticking up through the sand into the water column, but they can drive themselves deep into the sand at any sign of disturbance. They make rather good eating, not only for shorebirds, but for humans too!

Sea kayaking

Summertime, and the world heads for the beach. Great if you want to share the seashore's bounty with a thousand friends, but not so good if you want to genuinely discover what the coast is like when we humans are not around. Amazingly though, even in the most crowded of nations, secluded bays inaccessible by land are often just minutes away if you have the wherewithal. By far the best tool for exploring is the sea kayak. Just to get the nomenclature correct, in English parlance a canoe or a 'Canadian' is paddled with a single-bladed paddle and has an open deck. A kayak uses a blade that's more like a giant cotton bud with two ends, and the boat itself has a closed cockpit. Just to confuse matters, the whole subject is usually known as 'canoeing', though most enthusiasts consider themselves to be 'paddlers'. There are many subdivisions and specialist areas – squirtboats, playboats, marathons and surf skis for example, but all we really need to worry about here are sea kayaks. They are sleeker and longer than river kayaks, with deck space and compartments for gear, extra clothing and food, and generally have a rudder at the back to make steering easier (it's manipulated by pedals inside the cockpit).

The sea kayak was designed millennia ago by the native people of the Aleutian Islands, Greenland and Alaska. It was designed to slice through waves, to power onwards irrespective of swell and high winds, and to take the paddler just about anywhere accessible by water. With a paddle, you are self-reliant, self-sufficient and able to choose exactly what your day will bring. Quieter and less polluting than jetskis and powerboats, the kayak is also the kind of silent green machine that animals will not take exception to sharing the seas with. In various adventures around the world I have had Dusky Dolphins riding at my bow and leaping over my deck, had frisky Sea Otters actually trying to get into the kayak with me (honestly!) and nearly been swallowed by a host of feeding Humpback Whales that didn't even notice I was there.

All this said, sea kayaking is not for the untrained or the faint-hearted. Before considering doing any extended trip in a sea kayak, it is vital to take a course in kayak proficiency. Even some of the world's most competent paddlers will very rarely take to the open seas on their own. In a tricky situation it's very difficult to fend for yourself, so try and go in groups of at least two or three boats. Always check the weather, prevailing wind and tides, never forget your lifejacket, and leave word of where you intend to head to and a check-in time with someone responsible.

The primary skill to learn is being able to paddle in a straight line, which can be harder than it sounds. A rudder will help with this, and in most sea kayaks, turning (unless executing a full turn) is not achieved through preferential use of the paddles, but with the rudder. To do this, the pedals inside the cockpit must be adjusted so that your legs are slightly bent, then push-and-pull movement of the feet is used to engage the pedals. When travelling through shallow water, launching the boat, or going out through surf the rudder can usually be dropped into the water or retracted by use of a line that runs from behind the paddler to the rudder itself.

PADDLIN'

The secret to paddling in a sea kayak is consistency; use a long, relaxed stroke with almost straight arms, which leaves the large muscles of the back and shoulders to do all the work. If you find one shoulder or arm is hurting and the other isn't; make sure your hands are spaced evenly on the paddle shaft with your elbows at right angles, and that the rudder is straight. Modern paddles are built to make best use of this type of effort, using ultra-light carbon fibre materials with smaller blades, creating less drag in the water so easing the strain on the paddler. If you look at a whitewater paddle, you'll see the blade is way bigger – built for power and speed – out at sea, however, it's a marathon and not a sprint. As a good rule of thumb, a decent paddler on a calm sea in a standard boat without too much cargo can average 3 knots (that's 1–1.15 nautical miles an hour, or about 3.5 mph) for long stretches of time – about the same as walking pace. An experienced paddler with a lighter, narrower boat should be able to manage a steady 5 knots without any trouble.

THE ESKIMO ROLL

Using your paddle and hips to flick yourself back up when your kayak is turned over is a vital technique to learn. Nothing makes you feel more like James Bond than deftly righting your kayak after getting flipped in heavy waters. Trust me though, you should learn this life-saving technique under supervision in the controlled conditions of a swimming pool or sheltered bay before you try it in freezing cold water, in high swell with a loaded sea kayak.

The basic manoeuvre is that once you're over, you lean forwards from the hips, pointing one end of your paddle towards the

bow (the front), then sit back with force, throwing your paddle over your opposite shoulder as if it were a shovel and you were digging a big hole. A wee flick of your hips, and you should completely right the boat. With a lot of practice, you should eventually be able to Eskimo roll a fully-loaded sea kayak, even without the use of your paddle. If it fails, though, you'll be down to the old failsafe – abandon ship!

KAYAKING KIT

If you have become sufficiently expert at sea kayaking to consider an extended trip, you need to think very carefully about what you can make do with – or more importantly what you can do without. There's generally room for two backpack-loads of stuff in one boat. I've not done trips of over a week without having stops to restock food, but with the right amount of planning, there's no reason you can't pack for very long expeditions. In the mid 1980s, Ed Gillet paddled from California to Hawaii, and several people have paddled across the Atlantic. As an idea for expedition starters, take a light tent or bivi bag, a sleeping bag, and a sleep mat. Then you can plan to cook either over a wood fire or on a small camp stove. Dehydrated food is always a good way of eating well and saving space, or you can just take some rice or pasta, and put some effort into catching fish.

Folding kayaks provide an ultra-portable way to explore watery worlds. The most popular of all is the Feathercraft K Light, which packs down to an absurdly light 16 kg, and can quite easily be carried in a backpack.

▲ Paddling through 'The Bitches', a ferocious tidal race off Pembrokeshire.

Selected beasties to spot at sea

Some of the most spectacular of our marine creatures are best approached by paddle-power. The wildlife you are likely to see whilst sea kayaking obviously depends on the time of the year, location and your luck, but there's a good chance you'll see something special.

ORCA The Holy Grail of kayaking encounters, seeing an Orca's huge black dorsal fin break the surface near you is truly one of the world's great wildlife experiences. It is usually a fleeting encounter, as the pod (the group of Orcas) will be on the move, and they travel so fast it's impossible to keep up with them. These toothed 'whales' are actually large members of the dolphin family. They are probably the most widespread of all cetaceans and they are found in all the world's oceans, though they prefer cooler waters. Each generally weighs about four tonnes (about the same as three Mini Coopers). They feed mostly on herring, though many individuals specialize in marine mammals such as seals and sea lions, and others will take sea birds, otters, squid, penguins and even other whales. As with other members of the dolphin family, vocalization and echolocation is very important in hunting and communication. They make a series of whistles and calls, as well as echolocation clicks.

BASKING SHARK The largest fish found in European waters, the Basking Shark is often described as a gentle giant, but it is a powerful animal that should not be approached too closely. It can measure a whopping 12 m in length and weigh twice as much as an Orca. Very little is known about these mammoth beasts, due to their pelagic (open sea-living) nature and very few juvenile Basking Sharks have ever been seen. In the summer, however, Basking Sharks come into British waters and are often found off the western shores of the UK, most reliably off Cornwall and the Isle of Man. Unlike whales that feed on plankton, they don't have baleen plates; instead, hundreds of minute teeth and 'rakers' in their gills strain plankton as sea water washes through them. It was once thought Basking Sharks hibernated in the winter as they just seem to disappear, but scientists have recently discovered that they actually dive down to feed on plankton as deep as 1,000 m underwater.

COMMON OR HARBOUR SEAL These seals tend to be found around our Eastern coasts, and have a much rounder, arguably prettier face than Grey Seals, with nostrils that meet at the base (forming a V or heart shape) and a spaniel-like snout. The coat is often mottled with spots and rings. There's an estimated 28,000 around our shores, and they must be one of our most adorable creatures, though they do look a little pathetic when hauled up out of the water! They pup in late spring and begin their moult soon after in the summer – rhythms that seem to make a lot more sense than those of their larger cousin, the Grey.

GANNET Dive-feeding Gannets have officially been declared Britain's most outstanding wildlife spectacle, and the world's largest breeding colonies are located in the British Isles. Nothing compares to seeing vast squadrons of these elegant fighter jet birds circling effortlessly, before dive-bombing the seas in formation, emerging with fish that never knew what hit them! Even better is the inevitable following encounter, as piratical Great Skuas torment the Gannets on the wing, trying to get them to drop their catch. The Gannet is our largest seabird with a 2 m wingspan. It's a glorious white streamlined beauty with a caramel-coloured head, wing-tips that seem to have been dipped in black ink, and keen blue eyes ringed with what looks like Cleopatra-style black eyeliner. Younger birds have much duller plumage, and it's not until their second year that they take on their most majestic coloration. Gannets feed by plunge-diving from up to about 30 m above the water; zeroing in on a fish just below the surface, they then fold their wings to their sides and knife down to enter the water like a torpedo. They hit the water at about 60 mph, and so have evolved pockets of air in their shoulders and neck to protect their brains and vital organs from impact injuries; they also lack nostrils and instead breathe through the bill. Two-thirds of the world's Gannets nest in the UK, particularly in the vast colonies of St Kilda, Bass Rock and Grasholm. While many other seabirds are undergoing serious declines, Gannets are on the increase throughout Europe.

GREY SEAL If you see a seal poking its head out of the water in the north or west of the UK, chances are it's a Grey. Look for a long, Roman nose with a clear gap at the base of the nearly parallel nostril slits. Greys tend to be larger than Common Seals, and have more uniform coat coloration. They tend to pup in late autumn when weather conditions are at their worst, moulting in the late winter. It's thought that this odd pattern might be a throwback to glacial times, when seals would pup on pack ice. Playful Grey Seals will pop their heads out of the surf to watch you, and will let you get really close – as long as you don't make eye contact. As soon as they realize you've seen them, they'll whip their back flippers up over their heads and disappear with an over-dramatic splash, only to pop up again behind you for a really good look! Take care not to harass seals, particularly not when they have young pups, and don't get too close to seal haulouts (places where seals haul out of the water to rest), as they will probably head straight for the waves, their chill time ruined.

Coasteering

Until recently, scrambling round the coastline by whatever self-powered means necessary was just something inquisitive folks did. Then someone gave the enterprise a rugged-sounding name, decided it needed a lifejacket, helmet and wetsuit, and started charging loads of cash for the privilege of doing what was once the most natural and intuitive of activities. This is not necessarily a bad thing – it's introduced thousands more people to the intimate pleasures of our dramatic coastline, and I'll be honest, in British waters the wetsuit is a great idea. Well-organized outdoor centres can offer an insured, safe and guided day out that takes you to the very best of places, and takes all of the strain out of organizing it yourself. However, with a bit of good planning and confidence in your ability in the water, a little coasteering is an activity you needn't have to pay for.

▲ *Grab some mates and get clambering!*

The most important thing to take with you is at least one friend and ideally more. The risk of hurting yourself or getting stuck is low as long as you exercise care and common sense, but it's still not worth going it alone. A full knowledge of local sea and weather conditions and the tide is also vital.

For kit, I usually use my 3 mm triathlon wetsuit, as it has great freedom of movement and is excellent for swimming and clambering. In mid-winter, however, you'll want at least 5 mm. Reinforcing the elbows and knees with neoprene caving pads, or even skateboarding pads, will save both the suit and you from a scraping on the rocks. On your feet, normal trainers will do, though a well-draining model is much better than a snazzy waterproof cross-country job (which will fill straight up with water and not empty). The safety kit of lifejacket and helmet are also important. Lifejackets restrict your movement and make swimming harder, but will save your bacon if you knock yourself out (your wetsuit offers a certain amount of buoyancy, but not enough to keep you afloat). A helmet (ideally a whitewater kayaking helmet) will help protect your precious melon from slips and falls, but always take as much care as though you were bare-headed! A nose clip is a good idea to stop water going up your nostrils, and a pair of swimming goggles or a mask can add an extra dimension to the coasteering experience if you're going to snorkel too.

An ideal stretch of coastline would be somewhere like Pembrokeshire or Cornwall, with rocky inlets and bays, low rocks close to the water that you can scramble over, and sea caves you can swim into and through. Always pay close attention to the tide and to where you've been to make sure you'll be able to get back safely if you need to turn around.

Whilst scrambling round the shore, and getting in and out of the water, your worst enemies are going to be barnacles and mussels – both of which can be sharp as razors.

Classic coastal critters

BRISTLETAILS These extremely primitive wingless insects can jump as much as 10 cm by flexing their abdomens. The nymphs develop slowly and may have up to nine moults spanning two to three years before they reach maturity. They continue to moult (and therefore grow) throughout their lives regardless of age. They tend to feed at night on algae, lichens and decomposing vegetation, and are more often found in damp places such as the rocks on coastal cliffs.

FULMAR These birds resemble gulls, but are in fact petrels, (seabirds with tube noses) and are more closely related to albatrosses. They're glorious flyers, soaring on stiff straightened wings, apparently delighting in their ability to hover on the updrafts that race up the cliff walls they nest on. Well, I say nest; in actual fact they lay their single white egg onto bare rock, lined with paltry bits of vegetable matter. However, what really sets the Fulmar apart is its ability to chunder its evil-smelling oily stomach contents as far as 2 m. This might sound like a bit of comedy, but having unwittingly climbed onto a ledge and disturbed a pair of Fulmars, I can assure you that it is just plain vile! Other birds attacked in this way suffer even more, as the oil can matt their feathers, which leads to impaired flying and swimming performance.

EIDER One of our largest and more beautiful ducks, the Eider is well known for the insulating properties of its feathers (used in duvets – or eiderdowns). The courting males have a hilariously fruity mating call, which sounds a little like Kenneth Williams going '*ooooh!*' They breed from April to June in northern England and Scotland, and can appear anywhere around the coast in the winter months.

OTTER The first thing to say is that European Otters that live by the coast are *not* Sea Otters – that is a totally marine species which is not found in Europe. Sea-going Otters here must wash their fur in fresh water regularly in order to maintain its quality. With the exception of those in the west coast of Scotland, otters are generally nocturnal, feeding on fish, eels and shellfish, though they are fierce predators (they are just huge weasels, after all) and may take frogs and water birds as well. Otters deposit sweet-smelling droppings known as spraint around their territories in order to mark the limits of their range.

CORMORANTS AND SHAGS These are among the most easily identifiable birds on the wing, big black shapes flapping ponderously along low over the waves with their long necks held out in front of them, and their shortish, pointed wings working hard to keep them airborne. The Shag is designed to live at the coast, dining on eels and other fish. Some individuals have been found to swim as deep as 45 m in search of food, and can eat over a third of their body weight every day. Their feathers are not waterproofed (which means retention of air bubbles doesn't hinder their diving), so Cormorants and Shags are often seen drying off, standing in the sun with their wings held open.

The Underwater world

Whenever anyone suggests to me that British wildlife is too familiar, too tame, too... boring, I tell them to buy themselves a diving mask. We have a startling variety of wildlife off our coasts, much of which will come as a genuine shock to Joe Public. Show any person in the street a photo of a 2 m Conger Eel, an Angel Shark doing a flying carpet impression over the seabed or a seahorse coiled around a piece of seagrass, and they'd never believe it was the UK. Our Atlantic waters are also home to a variety of large predators, including the Thresher, Blue, Porbeagle and Mako sharks, and there is a even a dive/fishing operator running shark-diving excursions off the Cornish coast. They have a good record for getting people into the water (albeit in a shark cage) with Blue Sharks.

Scuba diving may be the ideal way to explore the underwater world, but it's expensive, proper training takes forever and when bedecked like a Christmas tree with equipment, I personally feel far too cumbersome to genuinely be a part of the environment. It's also a sport that usually imposes an age limit on those taking part. Snorkelling, on the other hand, offers anyone with a mask a window on another world, and any self-respecting adventurer can train themselves to hold their breath for a minute or more, giving them a free ticket to submarine paradise. Snorkelling was my parents' best method of getting a quiet time when we were kids; hand me a mask and I would disappear for the rest of the day, until sunburn, salt sores and exhaustion finally brought me back at sunset.

SNORKELLING

First, some techniques. To prevent your mask fogging, spit in it, or wipe it with washing up liquid, goggle drops, or – believe it or not – a slice of fresh potato! Then rinse the mask out. With your snorkel fitted to the mask strap and angled backwards at a 45-degree angle, the snorkel top should be out of the water and you should be able to breathe calmly and easily. When going into a duckdive, swim forwards quickly but under control,

then when you have momentum, jackknife at the waist so your head is now heading down, and bring one leg up in a straight line with the rest of the body. Gravity will sink you like a stone, then you have to kick to keep diving. As you go deeper, remember to 'equalize' pressure in your ears by pinching your nostrils shut and gently blowing (with your mouth shut). Do this often, and before pressure starts to become evident. When coming up to the surface, tilt your head back just before surfacing and breathe out. As long as you don't breathe in again until the snorkel is above the water, this will clear the snorkel of water using gravity. It requires far less effort than just huffing the water straight out vertically, is less likely to leave an annoying bit in the snorkel, and doesn't make a racket that may scare away wildlife.

Beautiful bubbles

Anyone dumb enough to want to rot their lungs with tobacco can blow a smoke ring, but how many can blow a shimmering, living, perfect bubble ring, which seems to be made of liquid mercury? Whales blow them out of their blowholes and sometimes even swim through their resultant masterpiece, seemingly for a bit of a giggle.

No wonder, they are surprisingly beautiful, and if you get it right, the ring will rise perfectly to the surface as if made of quicksilver. First take the biggest breath you can, then sink yourself down to the bottom. Flip on your back and get good and settled; the less turbulent the water is, the better your chances are. Let your mouth fill with air from your lungs, stick your tongue partially out and against your top lip, then blow a short raspberry with a sort of 'thub' sound. With practice (perhaps in the deep end of your local swimming pool), you could get a bubble ring as perfect as this one.

Do use a little common sense though. When I discovered the wonder of bubble rings I spent the following two hours diving down to sit on the bottom of the pool making them, only giving up when I nearly blacked out from lack of puff!

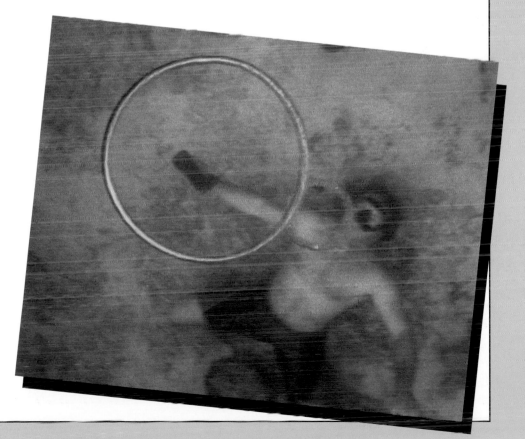

UNDERWATER SIGHTS

Getting underwater, whether it's on the Great Barrier Reef or off the coast of Plymouth, is all about seeing wild animals in their own world – a world which is totally alien to us. While we have deserts, forests and mountains, the marine world has its own different environments, and different animals that specialize in them. Kelp forests hide more animals than any woodland, sandy sea beds are home to flatfish, crabs and worms, reefs and wrecks offer sanctuary to larger fish and eels such as the giant Conger. Seagrass meadows are the best places to see seahorses, pipefish and cuttlefish, while the deeper seas form by far the largest habitat on earth and are home to species you will probably never see – except on your dinner table or in a natural history documentary.

LIGHTBULB SEASQUIRT
Unbelievably, aggregations of these little animals really do look like collections of light bulbs bobbing about in the current. They form colonies of 20 or so individuals (each about 2 cm long) joined at the base by a common 'root', which attaches to the rock they live on. The white lines on the sea squirts really seem to glow, particularly against dark backgrounds.

SPINY AND SHORT-SNOUTED SEAHORSES Our two rare species of seahorse are stupendously difficult to see, but well worth the effort in trying. They are actually bony fish, and like other fish they breathe through gills and have a swim bladder. Watching one feeding is like watching a high-powered Hoover suck tiny crustaceans from the water column, and if you listen carefully, you can hear an audible pop as it sucks in its lunch!

Probably the most fascinating fact about seahorses is that they undergo a 'reversed pregnancy', with the female transferring her eggs to the male for him to fertilize and care for in his pouch. Other interesting creatures that can be found lurking in seagrass include pipefish, crabs and cuttlefish.

ANGLERFISH This is a real weirdo of a fish, highly prized for its meat. The camouflage is exceptional, so you may well swim past even quite sizeable animals. Of course this is exactly what the Anglerfish is hoping its prey will do. The foremost spine of its dorsal fin is detached, and swings over its head to act as the angler's fishing rod – the fleshy tip is a lure that tempts smaller fish towards the cavernous mouth and doom.

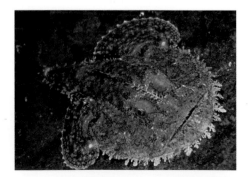

WOLF FISH These cold-water creatures are often found in deep, deep seas, but I've also seen them often on dives around the coast in far shallower waters. You usually see a fierce, snaggle-toothed head sticking out of a small cave, from which they'll dart out to munch down urchins and crabs. An individual will inhabit the same little hole throughout the summer, but move into deep waters in the winter.

COMMON SUN STAR This starfish's body has eight to thirteen rays, and is covered all over with small spines. If you flip a starfish over, you will see a groove running down the underside of each ray, and maybe – if the animal hasn't withdrawn completely, you may see hundreds of sticky tube feet protruding from the groove. These are used for locomotion and can be regenerated if they

get damaged or severed – in some species they will even grow into a new starfish! There are no hard mouth parts to capture prey; often the animal will prise apart prey such as molluscs using its limbs, before throwing up its stomach over its food, and covering it in digestive juices. When the tissues of the prey starts to break down, the starfish sucks it, and its stomach, back in.

SCALLOPS Scallops are bivalve molluscs (with a two-part shell) like mussels, clams and oysters. They are notable for their ability to swim, which they do by spurting out water to propel themselves forward. Should an inquisitive predator like a starfish come too close, the scallop can clap its shells together with enough force to drive it away at decent speed and for several metres. They use a rocking motion to make a hollow in sandy seabeds, and gape slightly to filter feed on particles in the seawater. Larger King Scallops are the ultimate prize for the coastal cook; nothing compares to the joy of spending a day diving for scallops then flash frying them up with a little bacon or chorizo – Jamie Oliver eat your heart out!

Know your whales

Dolphins, porpoises and whales comprise a group of mammals known as the cetaceans. If you want to sound like you know your stuff, slip into conversation the fact that they all evolved from a land-living ungulate (hoofed) mammal millions of years ago, and still have the remnants of the physiology that allowed them to live on land. These highly intelligent animals tend to have quite complex social lives, feeding together, then stopping to mess around, before all going into travelling mode in a group. Encounters with wild cetaceans are highlights for most marine naturalists.

MINKE WHALE I guess most people are familiar with the difference between a toothed and a baleen whale. In case you're not, the latter catches tiny prey such as krill by straining it out of the water using plates of hairy baleen that hang from the jaw. In UK waters we get the world's second largest baleen whale, the Fin, and also the smallest, the Minke (pronounced 'minkey'). Minkes are much more common and more often seen, and are set apart by the blue-grey body, the curving of the back moving through the water, and the comparatively small but distinctive curved dorsal fin. They're most often seen alone, cruising quite slowly, and are much bigger than any of the dolphins.

COMMON DOLPHIN There are five species of dolphin found in British waters, but the most common is... the Common Dolphin; who'd have thought it! It's found along the west coast and in the North Sea, is dark grey with a white underside and yellow markings along the sides of the body, and is very likely to ride the bow wave of boats.

BOTTLENOSE DOLPHIN The Atlantic Bottlenose is what everyone thinks of when the word dolphin is mentioned – the bright, smiley-faced 'Flipper' character that has charmed millions over the years. Bottlenoses are seen more often than other dolphins in British waters, being gregarious, and often keeping large social groups. They're a good deal larger than the Common Dolphin, reaching nearly 4 m, and are famously abundant in Cardigan Bay and the Moray Firth, where they're known to breed.

HARBOUR PORPOISE The only porpoise found in British waters is the Common or Harbour Porpoise. Generally speaking porpoises are differentiated from dolphins by their smaller, stubby bodies, and blunt, beakless faces. The dorsal fin is smaller and more triangular. The Harbour Porpoise tends to keep to small groups, is very active and up to 2 m long.

Fossil hunting

Lyme Regis and Lulworth Cove have a reputation on a global scale for fossils, but there are places all over the UK where they can be found. Don't get over-excited and head out with a rock hammer and a hard hat just yet though – the odds against you digging up a T Rex are fairly overwhelming. However, when climbing, caving or even just wandering along the beach, your chances of coming up with fossilized ancient shells is very good indeed; some of them are incredibly beautiful, and give you a glimpse of a prehistoric world.

A fossil is any evidence of prehistoric life that's been preserved in natural materials. They're usually found in sedimentary rocks such as those formed from accumulations of mud and silt. The classic fossil-finding site centres around an ancient river estuary, where plant and animal remains have been covered with the silt being poured out over millennia.

Trace fossils show the activity of ancient creatures – a classic example would be lines of dinosaur footprints in uncovered mud flats. Body fossils are the remnants of all or part of an animal or plant; usually the skeleton in the case of the former, which fossilizes more readily than the faster-decomposing soft body parts. The best body fossils result when the organism in question is sealed off quickly from elements that promote decay (such as oxygen), and kept secure from the physical elements of destruction such as erosion. Hard body parts such as bone and shell are actually porous with lots of tiny holes, allowing fine grains of minerals to get into them, replacing the original material in a process known as permineralization. Because of this, these fossils are much heavier than the original would have been – they're effectively animals turned into stone.

The main skill in ferreting for fossils is being able to tell random mineral swirls and fractures in rocks from things that were once alive. The best way to do this is to get yourself a book focusing on specific kinds of fossils, or head to a nearby museum that may have a selection of fossils from the area you're searching in. The next tricky bit is finding places where sedimentary rock is exposed at the earth's surface; such sites are easiest to find on coastlines where erosion is continually wearing rock away and unveiling old stuff. When working at the coast beware of all the things I've mentioned before in terms of tides and weather, but also take great care if working near to the edge of cliffs.

As with so many aspects of natural history, once you're aware of fossils, they can totally change your appreciation of the environment, whether you're out looking for them or not. I've only actually gone out specifically looking for fossils a couple of times in my life, but I've found some great ones when I've been caving, beachcombing and climbing. Always remember, though, that fossils are part of a country's heritage, and there is not an infinite amount of them out there. Collect sparingly and wisely – it's much better to take photos rather than specimens – and if you come up with anything you think may be of significance, contact a local museum.

A sieve is a good way of sifting out fossils from soft clays and silts, a paintbrush will help to remove dirt and dust from fragile specimens, and a hand lens or magnifying glass will greatly aid your examination of specimens. All this plus a helmet to protect your noggin, and a notebook and pen to record details of your finds, and you're on your way!

Cooking by the sea

Trying to eke a living from the land is a tough old business, but coastlines are like a free all-you-can-eat buffet, with an embarrassment of riches if you know where to look. It should be said right from the outset that collecting wild food must be undertaken in great moderation, with knowledge, care and regard for the natural environment. Many theoretically edible wild plants and animals are protected species and must be left alone, and you mustn't collect wild food of any kind from private land without the landowner's permission.

Mussels are the most obvious and easiest source of protein to be found at the seashore. They are, however, filter feeders and accumulate waste material found in the water in their tissues, so don't go collecting any bivalves next to sewage outflows. Only take the largest of the crop, and make sure they resist being opened whilst alive. Remove the beards, and cook them in fresh water – they must open up slightly when cooked or they're no good. Winkles (which look like snails), whelks, cockles and even limpets can be gathered and eaten (get rid of the runny orange guts and just eat the chewy muscular part). If you're very quick, you can tap limpets with a stone and knock them off their rocks, or even slip a knife under their skirts. Take too long though and they'll clamp down. Cooked limpets should just slide out of their shell; if they don't they need longer cooking.

Razor shells can be gathered from the sands at very low tides by taking a bucket of sea water and splashing it into their holes or by squeezing a washing up liquid bottle of salty water down there – they'll react as if the tide has come in and pop up above the surface. Grasp them tightly and wait a while for them to exhaust themselves. Then just chuck them into the fire – just three or four will provide a whole meal's worth of protein, and they taste superb.

Some of the best eating seafood caught from shore include prawns, mackerel cooked on the open fire, shrimp caught using a shrimp trap and crabs caught using lines baited with bacon or smelly fish. You can cook food in a sand pit – cover the pit with hot embers and cook food for an hour. As ever, take great care with anything involving fire.

Don't neglect the tasty seashore vegetables. Samphire and Rock Samphire are unrelated and grow in different habitats but both can be eaten. The fleshy-leaved greens have a crispy texture to them and – surprise, surprise, a salty flavour! Both are pretty pungent raw, and even when cooked should be taken in moderation. Steaming a fish inside Rock Samphire is an excellent way of providing the greens without them becoming overpowering. Sea Beet is a rather untidy looking plant – ancestor to our own beets and spinach, it is a rich source of iron, while Sea Purslane was once used by sailors to stave off scurvy. Sea Rocket can be found along sandy or stony beaches and has succulent leaves that can be eaten raw.

Sea Kale looks like a big cabbage, and is often found on stony shores. The leaves are too tough to be eaten, except as shoots, but side roots can be dug up (be sure to leave the main root intact so the plant will survive). The roots are of substantial size – they can be eaten raw, and provide a good source of sugary carbohydrate, with more calories than potatoes. The king of foraging, Ray Mears, names Sea Kale as being one of the best wild foods to be found in Europe, and thinks this could have been one of Stone Age man's most important foods. Chucked into the embers of a fire, it bakes delightfully.

MOUNTAINS

Britain's upland areas are our finest remaining wilderness, and the pride of our national parks system. Mountains are the grandest and wildest places for anyone to explore, and a whole host of plants and animals make their homes in our loftiest spaces. It's worth remembering, though, that the views we see here are not 'natural'. Many centuries ago all but the very highest peaks would have been wooded. A long history of clearance and grazing has formed the landscapes we see.

Magic mountains

Some of my finest wildlife experiences anywhere in the world have been in the modest mountains of Britain. I'll never forget seeing my first Golden Eagle, swooping so low over my head that the sound of its wings was like a gusting hurricane! Little compares with seeing Common Buzzards riding thermals, being harried by angry and insanely brave birds as small as Meadow Pipits, or a stooping Peregrine – one of the world's fastest creatures – smacking a pigeon out of the sky. And then there are those moments that will be etched on the brain forever – watching the sun rise over our deepest lakes from the summit of Scafell, plunging into an icy tarn in the Highlands after searching for Dotterels in the Cairngorms, coming to a ledge on a long rock climb to find myself eye to bright blue eye with a Jay standing by its nest, cocking its head at me as if to say, 'What d'you think you're up to, then?'

While such species are the archetypal sights of our uplands, during the summer months there are some visitors to the uplands that are more often associated with the coast. Curlews, Golden Plovers and Dunlins are all wading birds that you can hear calling across high moorlands during their summer nesting season.

The mountain environment creates great challenges for the animals that live there. For every 200 m of altitude gained in the hills, the temperature drops by approximately one degree Celsius. Night times are colder than at sea level, and rainfall is higher as rising air condenses against high rock. Areas like the Lake District and Snowdonia, where moisture-laden air comes in off the sea, are the wettest parts of the UK. Each year Snowdonia gets a third the sunshine and six times the rainfall as nearby Llandudno, which is at sea level.

In order to explore the mountains and see their special wildlife up close, you're going to need some serious clobber in terms of clothing and footwear, as well as a good degree of preparation. An intimate understanding of the weather and navigation are essential if you intend to spend much time in the hills, as climatic conditions can change very quickly up high. In the words of Billy Connolly: 'Mountain Rescue are sick of saving people halfway up Ben Nevis in khaki shorts and sand shoes.' Every mountain in Britain is an easy slog on a clear sunny day, but take a wrong turn in the fog somewhere like Crib Goch ridge on Snowdon and things can get very nasty. Get prepared, or sooner or later you'll get yourself in a pickle.

Anyone serious about becoming versed in the business of being a mountain man or woman should consider going on a Mountain Leader course, run by a company like Plas Y Brenin (the National Mountain Centre) or one of the outdoor centres in Aviemore. I'll touch on some of the essentials of navigation, weather and kit here, but there's really no substitute for experience and training. It's worth investing the time and effort to do it right. Anyone who is holding off on getting into the hills (perhaps wary of the weather) just needs to experience for the first time how much better their sandwiches and flask of tea taste on a hard-won summit. No high-class restaurant on the planet can match a squished pasty that's been earned on a hard hill yomp!

Navigation

I know what you're thinking: 'Maps and compasses are for old-fashioned beardies who don't know how to work sat-nav.' Well, this may be true, but I have several GPS systems myself, and have still had several situations where being a competent navigator has actually saved my life. For example, yomping up Ben Nevis at the end of 24 hours on the go, GPS batteries dead, visibility down to zero, a friend wanted to take the obvious route upwards. My map and compass told me that this would have taken us straight over Five Finger Gully; a mistake that kills people every year on the Ben. After sticking with what my compass told us, we were on the top within 15 minutes, instead of being the next statistic for the Lochaber Mountain Rescue (one of our nation's greatest institutions, by the way.) In addition, simple navigation can save you loads of time when you want to move quickly, and can be a great way to check or back up the info your modern technology may be giving you (or not giving you if it breaks or has no signal or power). No mountain qualification will even look at you without solid navigation skills.

The first and most important skill of navigation is *continuous map reading*, the intuitive skill of just following your progress on a map. As you travel, you should mentally tick off all the features around you from their relevant description on the map, and likewise anticipate the arrival of features on the ground. Trust your experience. If the map says you should have passed a stone wall and you travel 100 m past where you thought it should be with no sign of one, it's time for a rethink.

'Handrails' are a godsend for the novice map-reader. Keeping to an unmissable feature such as a large road, a stream or a dry stone wall can save you enormous amounts of time. They're great to fall back on in moments of strain as well; in poor visibility, at night, even when I'm just exhausted, I'll often travel twice as far as necessary in order to stay with a 100 per cent certain handrail. After all, nothing can match the frustration, the time wasting, the energy-sapping cluelessness of getting lost.

MAPS

The first thing you need to know about maps is their scale. Ordnance Survey maps are typically 1:25,000 (Explorer series) or 1:50,000 (Landranger series). This means that one centimetre on the map is equal to 250 or 500 metres on the ground. 1:25,000 covers a smaller area, and is therefore a much more detailed map and best for walking, whereas the greater distance covered by 1:50,000 maps makes them better for cycling or extended trips. Also, the compression of the larger maps makes features such as hills and valleys appear much more obvious on the map than they might prove to be in reality.

Maps are crisscrossed with grid lines running north to south and west to east. They will either be marked with Grid Reference numbers, or northings and eastings, which correspond to lines of longitude and latitude. In order to find a six-figure grid reference, follow the bottom line of the map until you find the square which corresponds to the first two figures of the reference. Then follow the vertical edge to find the square marked by the fourth and fifth numbers of the reference. The third and sixth numbers mark the precise location inside that box. You can use the roamers on your compass (the leading edge that's marked into smaller divisions) to find the exact location of a spot inside the relevant box. On a 1:25,000 map, this will give you a 100-metre square box in which to find a particular feature. A modern GPS should be able to give you this grid reference, though make sure it is referring to the same map you are.

The most essential aspect of map-reading ability is to be able to look at a map and make the weird orange lines and bizarre symbols come to life – to be able to make them three-dimensional in your mind. The key to this is contour lines. If they're tight together then the ground is steep. Widely spaced and the ground is nearer to being flat. Reading the elevation numbers next to each contour line should enable you to figure out if the feature you're looking at goes up or down. This simple detail spells the difference between two identical formations of contour lines describing a valley or a hill.

THE COMPASS

Being a bit of a mountain nerd, I always have a compass on me. Often I have two: one on my watch, and a wee button compass attached to my rucksack. For simple continuous map-reading, I just lay the compass down on the map and orient the map until north matches up. All of a sudden, every feature in the landscape should be in the logical direction indicated. However, the best choice for proper mountaineering is a flat compass with a clear base-plate, rotating bearing dial, direction of travel arrow and roamers (shown on the right). If you're going to be walking on a bearing, or doing any serious orienteering, these features are essential.

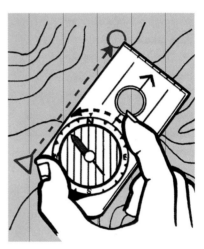

FINDING NORTH Well, that's easy, isn't it? It's the way the needle points on your compass. Well... annoyingly, no, it isn't. Unfortunately magnetic north is affected by the sloshing about of molten rock in the Earth's core, and the position of actual north and grid north are actually drastically different. Depending on where on earth you are, this 'magnetic variation' differs. It'll be shown on your map – here in the UK it's about four degrees, but this changes too!

The tricky part is reminding yourself whether you should add or subtract these degrees when taking a bearing. The simplest way of remembering this is that the landscape is bigger than the map, so the bearing number should be larger when applied to the ground than that on the map. So if you take a bearing off the map (let's say 210 degrees), you have to *add* the degrees (so it becomes 214 degrees), and if you take a bearing from the view, you should *subtract* it when applying it to the map (206 degrees).

To follow the compass and get an accurate bearing, hold it dead flat in front of you, and away from anything metal that might interfere with the needle. Unfortunately, metal-rich rocks can do this too, as I found out to my cost on the top of the Glyder mountains in Wales in a full-on white out – my compass was literally spinning from side to side! My advice in this situation is to give up and start crying like a baby (I did). Anyway, if you have the compass aligned correctly from the map, the direction of travel arrow on the bezel should now show you the way to go!

TAKING A BEARING OK, so you have a good idea of where you are on the map, and you want to head in the direction of a certain feature you can see on the map – let's say a church. Align the map so it's pointing north first so everything makes logical sense. Now use the compass's leading edge as a ruler, and draw a line between your location and the church on the map. Now line up the direction lines on the bezel with the north to south grid lines on the map. Add the degrees for deviation, and then follow the direction of travel arrow.

Backbearings are used when you can see certain features on the landscape that make sense, but don't know where you actually are. I'll be honest, this is a technique you will rarely use in mountain navigation, but it does help to cement your skills. If you're lost enough to need to take a backbearing, chances are you won't be able to see anything to take the bearing from... Point your direction of travel arrow at the feature – the church again. Then line up the bezel direction lines with the north-facing needle. Now subtract the magnetic deviation. Placing the compass flat on the map with the leading edge as a ruler, you can draw a line from the church. You are somewhere on that line. Repeat this whole process with another feature or two, and your position will be where the lines you draw intersect on the map.

DISTANCE TRAVELLED There are many methods of tracking your distance travelled, all of which are essential skills. However, they are all quite complex, and follow various rules depending on whether you're going up or downhill. For now, it is enough that you should think in terms of a given distance. Walk 100 m on the flat and see how many paces it takes you, and how long it takes. Then you can use this as a rough estimate when on the move. If you're expecting a road on the map to turn up within 100 m and you've done 300 paces without seeing it... you're not where you think you are.

When planning your day, you can expect to walk between 4–6 kilometres an hour (that's four to six squares on a 1:25,000 map) if you're reasonably fit, on flat ground, without a load and feeling fresh. Obviously this figure can change wildly depending on these and other factors. On a recent expedition hacking my way up a knife-edged ridge with a heavy load, we managed just 10 metres an hour!

One last word – if you find things are not adding up to what you expect to see on the map, *go back* to your last known point of location. If the contours on the map go downhill and you're going up, if you pass a road that shouldn't be there, if you are expecting pylon wires and they don't appear... Go back! I am terrible at this, always thinking: 'I'll just push on, bound to find something...'. I never do. You will always waste less time by being careful and going back. If only I could practise what I preach...

Sensing the weather

One of the best ways of staying out of trouble – or at least comfortable – in the mountains, is having a rudimentary knowledge of what the weather's likely to be doing the day you're out, or at least for the next few hours. We all know the old saying, 'red sky at night, shepherd's delight, red sky in the morning shepherd's warning'. This is quite often true; red sky at times of low sun often means the weather in that direction is generally settled.

Animals are often much better at predicting weather than we are, and watching them can be a great way of keeping up to speed. I'll never forget sitting outside on a seemingly fine summer's evening, watching bats pour out of the eaves of a house they'd been roosting in, off for an evening's foraging. Not half an hour later, the bats all poured back in again leaving us totally mystified… until moments after the last bat was safely home, when the heavens opened, having us all vainly scarpering for shelter from the downpour.

While we can never emulate the sixth sense animals seem to have, the good adventurer spends enough time outside to become reasonably in tune with his or her environment. Most of the lore of old farmer's and sailor's almanacs has its basis in good scientific fact. Everything seems sharper as a storm approaches, because air pressure drops and dust particles in the air fall. Bird calls are audibly clearer, and they may fly even closer to the ground in the search for insects on the wing; both birds and bats prefer the denser air lower down as pressure falls. With high pressure and dry air they'll be back up high again. Birds stuff themselves and roost early and dandelions fold their petals before heavy rain.

Anyone can sense the approach of a tropical storm through its characteristic heavy smell and the indescribable oppressive feel to the atmosphere, but given time you can sense even small showers through a certain fresh clarity of the air. I've spent a lot of time living with hunter-gatherer peoples who are so tuned in to their environment that they will down tools without a word, walk home, and step into their snug shelter just seconds before a downpour.

When campfire smoke starts to spiral about and drop to the ground, low pressure is on the way. Likewise, people who complain of old war wounds playing up before storms are not as bonkers as they sound – it's due to falling pressure allowing gas inside our bodies to expand. Crickets and grasshoppers loudly stridulating (that's a clever word for insect singing) is a good sign of sustained good weather, and the presence of loads of gossamer (spider's silk) over bushes on a fine morning also indicates the good weather is there to last.

CLOUDS

Now for a wee science bit (stick with me here). Earth's atmosphere is made up of several distinct layers, the lowest of which is the troposphere. When air ascends, it cools at a rate that depends on whether it's 'dry' – without clouds – or 'saturated.' As the air rises, it moves into a part of the troposphere that has lower pressure, so it expands and cools. Clouds are produced by this cooling, which causes water vapour to condense into cloud droplets – or ice particles in the right circumstances. Warm air can hold more water vapour than cold air.

Whilst the troposphere is repeatedly mixed, the next layer up – the stratosphere – is much more stable. The temperature here is much more constant, and it is much drier. In contrast to the troposphere, it is warmer at the top of the stratosphere, and cooler below.

If you start out a big day in the hills under blue skies, with high and white clouds, all is good! However, if small, low, scattered cumulus (round, fluffy clouds) start to appear, it's time to start paying attention. If these clouds start to grow upwards quickly, it indicates the upper troposphere is unstable, and there's a really good chance of rain. If they are deep, dark and reach the top of the troposphere, heavy rain and thunder are likely. Generally, these black thunder clouds are unmistakable. If the cumulus remain shallow, precipitation is less likely.

The one thing we all want to avoid is a large incoming storm, which sends all sorts of different signals. The clouds and winds will be changing dramatically in direction and intensity. Smaller storms give less warning and may well appear out of nowhere and be gone again just as fast. This may be preceded by wind, but if rain starts to fall with little change in wind intensity, the weather system may well be around a lot longer. The formation of very high clouds, such as cirrus, can herald the arrival of a warm front. If the cirrus is followed an hour or so later with thicker cirrostratus or cirrocumulus this is a good sign, and you can expect a good day out!

The difference between areas of high and low pressure across the Earth's surface drive the winds, which move clouds and weather systems around. One of the best ways of tracking pressure changes and using them to predict the weather is a barometer – I have one on my watch. Falling pressure can indicate the approach of a warm front or a depression, and a rise can indicate the presence of a cold front.

▲ There's truth in the old proverb: a red sunset can be a sign of good weather on the way, but a fiery red sunrise may herald unstable weather.

▲ Many invertebrates, such as this Bush Cricket, can predict the weather better than a modern barometer.

▲ If the sky looks like this, pack your bags and head for the hills!

Become a mountain monkey

Admittedly, I have a certain bias when it comes to getting outdoors. If the weather will allow it, chances are I'm going to be out climbing. There are a lot of reasons for this, but the most important is that climbing takes you away from the realms of the normal walker or tourist, and gets you into a place that only the experienced can taste. Being able to climb has given me the chance to undertake some of the most serious expeditions on the planet, and see animals and places that no other human being has ever seen. At the same time, it has also given me the joy of being able to test myself physically whilst having control over my own fate. People who think climbers have a death wish and are deliberate risk-takers have it all wrong; it's the opposite, it's about control. Climbing is about having faith in your own abilities to conquer danger through experience and skill. It is about giving people back control over their own destiny. Anyone who thinks this sounds melodramatic should sense the exhilaration of topping out on a route that's really tested them to the limits, turning around at the top and seeing a once familiar view from a totally different perspective. That's what climbing is about.

With climbing comes elevation, and a fine opportunity to view our most dramatic birds of prey. I've often hung in a belaying stance or leaned back to chalk my fingers high up a mountainside and had Peregrines, Common Buzzards or crows such as Choughs actually soaring below me. In stark contrast to the way we usually see such birds, silhouetted against the sky, you can see their colours to full effect and appreciate even more their mastery of the updrafts and the winds.

There's whole host of different types of climbing, but certainly the ones that give you the best chance of getting into wild territory are scrambling, traditional climbing and mountaineering.

SPORT CLIMBING

This sport is gaining popularity all over the world, here in the UK largely due to the mass advent of indoor climbing walls. Sport routes are sections of rock that have metal bolts drilled into them (fixed either with expansion bolts or hard drying resin). The lead climber clips his rope through runners or quickdraws attached to the bolts – the rope then runs down to the ground and to his partner, the belayer. It's the safest form of climbing outside, but there are comparatively few routes here in the UK, and they tend to be well trammelled, so not much cop for wildlife spotting.

BOULDERING

This is the form of climbing for which you need the least kit (just a pair of climbing shoes really), but again is unlikely to bring you into close contact with wild animals. Boulderers just find chunks of rock that are not so big they'll mind falling off them, and find a variety of routes to the top. It's superb training, as it requires precision, power and balance, and many would claim it is the most pure form of climbing. As you are often deliberately seeking out the hardest way of getting to the top of something, I think it's also the most artificial.

Climbing techniques

It doesn't matter which avenue of climbing you're going to be exploring, the basic principles are always the same, and a few simple bits of advice can make all the difference to your abilities.

The muscles of the legs and backside are the largest and strongest in the body, used to carrying around your bulk all day long. The muscles of your forearms and hands are comparatively tiny. If you try (as blokes always do when they first start climbing) to drag yourself up a climb by a series of chin-ups, you will exhaust yourself almost immediately. Girls on the other hand usually lack the macho 'sprint at a problem headfirst' gene, and instinctively climb using more balance and their legs and feet. This is why you see countless couples turning up to climbing walls for their first try at climbing, and the guy being left steaming with frustration as his girlfriend easily outdoes him.

Generally speaking, the best way to travel upwards is to make sure one foot at least has a solid foothold, then shift your bodyweight so it is above that leg, then stand up.

Precision is also vital in climbing. Wasted energy can be disastrous, so every time you make a decision, such as where you're going to put a toe, look straight at the hold and watch it right until the move has been made. Likewise with clipping your rope through runners; look at the hand that has the rope and watch it right up until the rope is secured. You'll be far less likely to miss and scrabble around for ages.

Indoor rock climbing is one of the fastest growing sports in the world, and while it certainly isn't going to get you any wildlife encounters, it is hands down the best way to learn rock climbing techniques. All I ask is that you don't get obsessed with indoor climbing to the exclusion of all else – plastic holds in climate-controlled arenas are the antithesis or what the real, outdoor climbing experience is all about.

TRADITIONAL OR FREECLIMBING

This involves climbing sections of rock – often very extended or multi-pitch – that have not been pre-prepared with bolts. Instead, the climber carries a selection of equipment (known as a rack) with camming devices, nuts, hexes and slings, which are placed into cracks in the rock, or otherwise used as improvised anchors. The climber then puts in runners or quickdraws, much as in sport climbing, and runs his rope back to his belayer below. This is the kind of climbing that is most likely to bring you face to face with a feral Wild Goat or a soaring raptor (and for this reason is often restricted during nesting season – check with local parks authorities).

Whilst free climbing I've watched our smallest bird of prey (a Merlin) bullying our largest (a White-tailed Eagle), and seen a stoat raiding a crow's nest for the chick inside. I've also had my sternest ticking off. On a thin ledge halfway up a long climb in Wales, I pulled a disposable barbecue out of my rucksack (to the shock of my climbing partner), and started cooking sausages. Minutes later, a giant mountain rescue helicopter came and hovered just metres in front of us to see if we were signalling for help! I'll never forget the stern finger-wagging the pilot gave me when he saw I was making lunch… As usual, please learn from my mistakes rather than emulating them!

The freedom 'trad' gives you is unparalleled. Once you have the skills and the kit you are a paid-up member of the explorer club, and with the right ambition can find yourself leading new routes in some of the most spectacular parts of the world.

SCRAMBLING

This is another excellent way of getting yourself into some of the most remote and wild places in the UK. Generally speaking, if you're needing to use your hands to get up a peak then you're scrambling, but most outdoors types would reserve the classification for such classic routes as the Cuillen Ridge on Skye, Crib Goch and Bristly Ridge up Glyder Fach. Scramblers do not carry any specialist kit like ropes, which offers the obvious benefits of simplicity and lightness, but this does also mean scramblers can potentially can get themselves into a lot of trouble if they get lost or out of their depth. Again, there is no substitute for experience.

Remarkable raptors

COMMON BUZZARD

A large bird with rounded wings which are often held in a shallow V as it glides, and with a short neck and tail. The classic view of a Common Buzzard is a broad-winged shape soaring over wooded hillsides, perhaps with a couple of crows noisily badgering the larger bird. These wonderful birds have shown just what superb survivors they are with a remarkable recovery over the last decade. They suffered terribly from the introduction of pesticides into the environment in the 1950s and 1960s but have made an extraordinary comeback, and have now superseded the Kestrel as our most common bird of prey. The superficially similar Honey Buzzard has fewer than 50 breeding pairs in this country, so if you see a bird that looks like a Common Buzzard... it's probably a Common Buzzard.

RED KITE

This is an unmistakable bird, incredibly graceful on the wing and the only British raptor with a deeply forked tail. Seen on the wing, you'll miss the vibrant red and silver-grey coloration, so definitely get out the bins and try and catch them when they're not silhouetted against a pale sky. I've lived a good portion of my life in the Chiltern Hills, and we Chilternites now tend to fondly think of the Red Kite as 'our' bird. Go out to the local hills any day of the year, and you're bound to see kites hanging impressively in the wind. These birds are evidence of one of the most successful reintroduction campaigns in British history, and Red Kite chicks are being taken from the Chilterns to set up new populations all over the country. Kites were probably persecuted to near extinction because they were seen by gamekeepers as a threat to gamebirds. However, the Red Kite is very unlikely to kill large birds, probably earning its bad reputation when it was seen eating already dead Pheasants.

GOLDEN EAGLE

When I was a kid, the Golden Eagle seemed the epitome of the wilds, the UK's most powerful and majestic predator. I didn't get to see one in the wild until my 20s but it was worth the wait. This huge bird looks like a flying surfboard! The massive beak doesn't kill, but is put to good use tearing a carcass apart; it's the huge talons that do the real dirty work. Having had a tame one sitting on my wrist, I can confirm that it felt like the talons could reduce my arm to shreds. Though the Golden Eagle has a reputation as a fearsome predator, it also gains food by scavenging carrion, and farmers may have poisoned or shot many birds after seeing them feeding on sheep carcasses. Golden Eagles do occasionally kill small lambs, but they would never take on a fully grown sheep. They mate for life, building a gigantic nest called an eyrie, which may be used for many years. Chick-feeding duties are shared, and the eagles may even work in tandem when hunting, driving prey towards their waiting partner. Until at least 2008 there was a solitary male holding territory at Haweswater in the Lake District, and around 430 breeding pairs in Scotland.

PEREGRINE FALCON

As a climber, I am especially familiar with Peregrines. They tend to inhabit wild rocky areas, quarries, sea cliffs, mountainsides, and their yickering call is often heard reverberating around rocky amphitheatres. The call has something of the Green

Woodpecker about it, but is much higher and more piercing. Sometimes it seems that Peregrines call constantly whilst on the wing, particularly when two adults are chivvying a youngster, forcing it to stay airborne in order to build its strength and confidence. As any small child will tell you, Peregrines are the fastest creatures on Earth – and this is all to do with their remarkable hunting method. The Peregrine feeds on birds on the wing, and will fly above them, before 'stooping'; folding its wings to its sides, and plunging like a torpedo down at its mark. They are said to reach 180 mph (some sources say 200 mph) at full speed, and obviously when they hit their target, the shock is so dramatic as to pretty much ensure a kill. However, as you'd expect, such a high-risk strategy means many missed targets. Peregrines have many adaptations to help them survive the high speed drop, including baffles in their nostrils, which allow them to breathe as they stoop – and presumably prevent them blowing their own brains out the back of their heads!

Carnivorous plants of the hills

Mountain environments offer special challenges, including loads of rain, and a lot less sunshine than other parts of the country. Also, all that rain can leach nutrients out of the soil, making life really hard for plants. Some plants have come up with rather neat (if slightly macabre) ways of supplementing their income of nitrates – by catching and eating insects. When we think of carnivorous plants, it's usually the fearsome Venus flytraps or giant pitcher plants of the tropics (some of which can even catch rats and frogs!). However, in this country we have three distinct types of plants that munch down bugs, and in their way, they are just as wonderful.

BUTTERWORT

These are characterized by rosette-shaped clusters of leaves, with sticky upper surfaces and a central stalk often topped by a pretty flower. Like the sundews, these plants form a tight bud called a hibernaculum which they retreat into during cold winters (almost like a hedgehog hibernating through the winter). Their technique for catching prey is perhaps a little more primitive; they don't seem to have a sophisticated method of attracting insects, but merely capture those that happen to land on them, with the leaves curling inwards to trap small invertebrates.

▲ *Innocuous looking Butterworts spell disaster for careless insects.*

BLADDERWORT

These are very peculiar plants indeed, having spindly stalks and generally growing with most of their bulk underwater in peaty pools. Below the surface, the floating stem has a system of air-filled transparent bladders, like little blisters, which actually snap up and digest the insect larvae that swim about in the water. Each bladder has little hairs that guide the prey towards the closed mouth of the trap. When the plant senses an insect is nearby, it snaps open the trap, and water rushes in to fill the vacuum,

▲ *Bladderworts prey on tiny invertebrates. Their microscopic murder is a marvel few will ever see.*

carrying the tiny unsuspecting insect in with it. Later on the bladder is pumped out in readiness for the next victim. When in flower they can be really beautiful, looking much like floating orchids.

SUNDEW

These bright red jewels, with tentacles topped with glistening globules of dew, look as if they've been made by pixie glassblowers! However beautiful, these little tentacles have a nefarious purpose, functioning just like sticky flypaper. Special glands secrete sweet nectar that attracts insects (like the damselfly above) to come and have a sniff. When the insect lands, the tentacles fold inwards, bringing the prey into contact with more of the sticky bulbs. The struggling insect eventually succumbs to exhaustion or asphyxiation, and then digestive enzymes start to break it down. The resultant goo is used by the plant as a food.

Top fell finds

DOTTEREL One bird that you may actually see on the ground is the Dotterel. These summer visitors come to the UK from North Africa to nest in places like the Cairngorms, feeding on the plentiful summer explosions of insects such as crane flies (and let's face it, in Scotland, midges). These birds are unusual in that it's the males who take care of the young, leaving the females free to go off and cheat on them with other males. Dotterel dads are so dedicated that you can get very close to them and they'll not flee the nest. Of course it goes without saying that you need to respect them and all other ground-nesting birds (in fact, it is illegal to disturb Dotterels and other rare birds at the nest), and don't stampede through heather and thick grassland in the nesting season.

CAPERCAILLIE
This grand and slightly bizarre bird is the largest member of the grouse family, and is particularly well known for its mating displays. A famous natural history film shows legend David Attenborough given absolutely no respect by a furious and territorial male Capercaillie in the full flush of passion – it ran right over him while the great man collapsed in giggles! The male is twice the size of the female, and a seriously impressive bird, more like a turkey than a grouse. The weird chuckling, gobbling courtship call also has something of the turkey about it, and is one of the most distinctive of all British bird calls; one which is only heard in the conifer forests of the Scottish Highlands, which the Capercaillie calls home. At the end of the courting season the males all assemble at leks (places birds have set aside to come and show off to the opposite sex), and perform, fanning out their tails and chuckling their crazy songs. The best place to see them is early morning at the RSPB's Loch Garten reserve.

PTARMIGAN The Ptarmigan is a type of grouse, very much associated with highlands and wild places. In the UK it is only found in the highlands of Scotland. It's famous for its seasonal wardrobe – mottled white and brown from spring to autumn, then snow-white to give it camouflage through the icy winter months. Although Ptarmigans can fly, they are more usually seen wandering about as if in absolutely no hurry, feeding on berries, seeds and occasionally insects. During the last ice age they would have made their homes throughout much of Europe, but today's milder climate has seen them banished to the coldest parts of the continent.

REINDEER Yup, believe it or not, Santa's sleigh draggers can be found right here in the UK! Once they would have roamed around all of our country naturally, but they died out around 8,500 years ago. In the 1950s, an enterprising rancher decided it was time they made a comeback, and set up a herd of around 160 animals, which now run semi-wild in the Cairngorms – perhaps our nation's wildest and most beautiful place. Famously feeding on lichen, fungi and whatever vegetation they can find in the austere environments they inhabit, Reindeer have a coat of long hollow hairs, underlaid with soft, denser fur, which makes a regular duvet for them to keep warm under. Their broad splayed feet, with hair in between the hoof halves, allow them to easily travel over snow and ice without sinking or slipping. They're yet another example of how re-introductions can make a wonderful complement to the wildlife of our nation. I just wish someone would listen to me and bring back bears and wolves!

Upland tracks and signs

While the mountains may not be as overrun with wildlife as the coasts or forests, they often have great substrates for picking up prints. Bare rock is obviously useless, but peaty boggy ground can hold a print as well as soft plasticine. If you want to preserve a print, maybe in order to examine it in more detail later on, the best way is to surround it with a deepish frame, perhaps made of a taped-up loop of firm card pushed firmly in place around the print, then fill the frame with liquid plaster of Paris. When it hardens, you can lift out the cast, and you'll have a perfect replica of the underside of the animal's foot.

RED DEER

All deer have two distinct halves or cleats to their hooves, the print being a broad oval shape, with the hind hooves being notably smaller than the front ones (and female prints smaller than those of the stags). Dewclaws are located high up the leg, and are never seen in prints, unlike those of, for example the Wild Boar. Interestingly, when the Red Deer is moving slowly, the rear foot prints will be placed inside those of the forelimbs, though when they speed up the prints are much more spread out. The native Red Deer is our largest land-based mammal, stags standing about 1.5 m at the shoulder. The size of the Red Deer is particularly relevant in October, when one of our finest wildlife spectacles takes place – the rut. It's now that huge stags, with full heads of antlers, battle it out to gain control of their harem of females. It's a fantastic spectacle, with the deer bellowing and charging at each other, with oodles of bluff and bluster. Eventually though, genuine clashes must occur, and they can be utterly brutal. Many stags are badly injured or even killed by these vicious collisions during the rut. This is one of the only times that one of our native mammals can actually be a potential danger to humans. The males can be territorial, aggressive, and very, very big!

BADGER

Badger prints look how I imagine little teddy bear tracks would look; there are four clear toeprints (and one less clear one) with claw marks, and a distinct central pad to the foot. The scat is rather dog-like; blunt-ended, and rarely seen in the colder months, as Badgers spend most of their time inside their setts, and use latrines underground. At other times they use communal dung pits regularly. These may occur near the main sett, or at the outer limits of their territory, and serve as an 'information station' for nearby Badgers to check out. Perhaps the best sign to look for is their large sett entrances, often dug into shallow slopes. There will be far more

▲ No, there's not been a teddy bear's picnic nearby, these are badger tracks.

excavated material around the entrance than seen in any other British species, and you may see their footprints in the soft sandy soil around the entrance. You may also find a scratching tree nearby – often for some reason an elder – its bark deeply scored or completely worn away up to a height of 1 m. Another great sign to look for is disturbance under manmade fences. You'll see a scraping of the earth, and there may be discarded hairs which are banded black and white.

When Badgers set to excavating, looking for underground prey, they create what are known as 'snuffle holes', with a central hole the Badger has been pushing its nose into, and a surrounding scuffed up area where it's been digging. Many people are surprised to find out that such a high proportion of the Badger's diet is made up of worms and insect larvae, though they may dig up the nests of mice, rabbits and other small mammals too.

WILD OR FERAL GOAT

The Wild Goat has scat that is quite sheep-like, drier and easier to break into pellets than that of other wild hoofed animals. The hoofmark is cloven, and very similar to that of sheep. However, Wild Goats are even more nimble climbers than sheep, and can be found in even the most precipitous of environments. Goats roaming wild in the UK are all the descendants of domestic goats, which at some stage escaped or were released. These often beautiful animals have been living in the wild here in the UK for so long now that I think they deserve re-branding. After all, 'Feral Goat' makes them sound like tramps or hobos. Think of a 'mountain goat' and you probably envisage an Ibex or Chamois – magnificent, dramatic, a symbol of the wild. Admittedly our own version may not have the spectacular horns of the Ibex, but they're still nimble-footed and comparatively rare; and I think deserving of much respect. They can often be spotted clambering on impossibly steep rocky ground in some of our nation's most mountainous regions. Check out the thick shaggy coats and the unkempt beards the males (billy-goats).

WILDCAT

Unfortunately, the chances of seeing a Wildcat are seriously slender! I've spent most of my life in the great outdoors in the UK and have never seen one. They're also hybridizing with feral domestic cats, so pure-bred Wildcats are as rare as hen's teeth. However, to actually track and find a genuine British Wildcat would be one of the UK's greatest experiences... if you manage it, write and let me know! One of Britain's very few remaining large wild predators, the Wildcat has been here for millions of years, but now there are probably no more than 400 left in the wild. Claw marks are usually absent from the tracks, and the cat may leave scratch marks in trees, and leave scent marks with urine or faeces.

Edible plants of the hills

The hills are relatively harsh places if you're wanting to go hunting for edible plants. Very few of the plants that occur exclusively in high places make good eating. However, there are plants of the lowlands that can also be found on lower slopes and valleys; if you're foraging, best not to head too high!

One of the familiar plants that we can all identify and that can be eaten is the common Daisy. The leaves don't taste great (they're a bit bitter) but they are OK in cooked foods, and contain as much vitamin C as lemons. You can also eat the buds and flowers. Both the leaves and roots of Dandelions are also edible (if a bit acrid). The leaves are great in a salad, and even better if slightly wilted in the smoke of a fire, or steamed.

All of the fruits and vegetables we see on show in our supermarkets have wild ancestors, and some of these can be still located in the British countryside. A perfect example is the Crab Apple. It's found throughout the UK, and favours sunny slopes. The fruits come out in the autumn, and are best cooked, as they are too bitter and tart otherwise. Baking them is ideal, wonderful if done with some honey or brown sugar.

My family was lucky enough to grow up surrounded by woodlands with an endless supply of wild fruit, and mum was an absolute whiz at making crumbles and pies from wild blackberries, apples, damsons and plums (though dad always used to claim responsibility – as he'd collected the fruit). However, with wild land shrinking by the day here, and many of us having much less opportunity to get out into the countryside, even finding such obvious fruits as these may be a difficult task.

Generally speaking it's going to be late summer onwards that wild fruits ripen. Brambles provide blackberries, often in huge amounts. There's a limitless variety of ways of cooking blackberries up, but of course in a survival situation you'd certainly not consider cooking them – just get as much of that valuable natural sugar down as you can stomach! Wild Strawberries are one of the first fruits of the year to come into season (in early June), and may continue providing fruit right through till September. They're much smaller than the monstrosities you get in supermarkets, but you'll never forget your first one – all of a sudden mass-produced strawberries will taste utterly artificial by comparison.

The wild Raspberry is (like the Bramble) armed with vicious spines to its stems, but it's worth a little tangle to get to the divine fruits. These have a tendency to grow in very damp soils, and are mostly found fruiting from late summer onwards.

One of the few truly upland plants that's actually good to eat is the Blaeberry, also known as Bilberry and Whortleberry (seen right). Found on moors and also on heathland, the Blaeberry is similar to the cultivated blueberry. The fruits are a rich source of vitamin C and are delicious straight from the bush or cooked in a pie.

FRESHWATER

Freshwater environments are a great place for an adventure naturalist to spend time. Whether it's a beautiful, clear, flowing river or a shimmering lake, there's always an abundance of wildlife to be found in and around water.

Watery wonders

When summer comes and things get a little hot under the collar, we all find ourselves being drawn to water like moths to a flame (or maybe to your ultraviolet moth trap if you're a keen naturalist). Not surprising really; our bodies are up to 80 per cent water, and whilst we can survive weeks without food, just a couple of days without water and we'd be goners.

One of the most basic things I remember from my biology studies is the water cycle – that all the water on the earth is finite, and has been enclosed within the Earth's atmosphere for millennia. Water falls from clouds as rain or snow, passes through the soil, through plants, through rivers and other bodies of water, and eventually evaporates back up to become clouds again, but the amount of water in the Earth's system never changes. As every organism in the world depends on water to survive, this fact is especially important. When we pollute water, we are ruining an essential part of the Earth's ability to function.

Freshwater environments are also extraordinarily exciting places. I took my kayak out for a long paddle on the very first day the mayflies erupted from the river – the air was choked thick with golden insects, bouncing and dancing in the sunlight, and then to my delight a Hobby starting hunting them – right over my deck. British wildlife just doesn't get any more ethereal than that! Many of the insects we see flying about our ears have spent the majority of their life as larvae under the surface of the water, avoiding the attentions of the numerous predators that choose to live there. Pond dipping and making your own wildlife pond can give you a chance to make a closer acquaintance with some of these And while you may only have thought of getting out the mask and snorkel down at the seaside, freshwater environments can be just as rewarding as places to go underwater searching.

Pond dipping

Every naturalist worth his or her salt should give pond dipping a try; it is one of the easiest and most rewarding ways of seeing bizarre water beasties. You'll need a stout net (tougher than a butterfly net or seaside crab net) with fine mesh. Most of what you will pick up will be pond weed and mud, and that's pretty heavy – a weak net will just fall apart.

The thing about pond dipping is that it's a game of chance; you're not aiming to catch a fish you can see, but sweeping about blindly for little critters lurking in the murk. Give it a while, and you're almost guaranteed to find some larvae (if they have a pupa stage between infant and adult) or nymphs (if they do not pupate but 'hatch' as adults straight out of their immature bodies), and they're so much more fascinating if you can identify them, and get to understand a little of what goes on in their lives, and what they will eventually become.

Pond dipping is really all about location. A good pond or lake in a nature reserve surrounded by lots of plants and with a lot of aquatic plants growing in the water is ideal (and many nature reserves offer pond-dipping days with identification help on hand) but you'll probably also get results out of a seemingly stagnant city pond full of ducks! The technique is simply to sweep the water at a variety of levels, but always going in one direction – the second you change direction with your net you'll lose everything that was in it. Once you've had a sweep, tip the contents into a container with water in it. A shallow white tray works best for analysing your finds. The small aquatic larvae found on murky pond bottoms are so numerous and so fascinating that I've given them their own special section (on pages 128 and 129), and have concentrated here on the really dramatic big stuff that'll make any pond dip memorable. The Great Crested Newt is included to give you an indication of what to do if you catch one accidentally – you should never intentionally capture one of these protected wonders.

It should be said straight off that the edges of any body of water are potentially dangerous, so don't go pond dipping on your own if you're a younger reader, and always use caution – stretching out way into the water to try and have a good dunk might get you some good results, but sooner or later it will also get you wet! If you're lucky, you might find some of these fellas...

GREAT RAMSHORN

As the name suggests, the brick-coloured shell of this magnificent snail is flattish and curled up like the horn of a ram. They feed on vegetation and algae, which can make them a great addition to a pond, as they'll help keep it clean. In the wild, Ramshorns will lay a cluster of eggs covered with jelly on the underside of submerged leaves, but in a wildlife tank they may well lay them on the glass, which allows you a perfect view as the young snails hatch out.

GREAT POND SNAIL

Easily told apart from the Ramshorns, the Great Pond Snail has a more rounded, greyish or yellowy-brown shell which curls backwards in a spiral (more like you would expect from a snail). It's the biggest pond snail in the UK, and can grow to be a real monster! The egg mass is kept within a long globule of jelly, and with practice can also be told apart from the Ramshorns' eggs. The feeding strategy is very similar, and they are another welcome addition to any natural water feature – as long as the water isn't moving much.

STICKLEBACK

Perhaps 50 years ago many a young kid would have kept a jar of sticklebacks in their bedroom, and watched in wonder as the males erupted in bright red breeding colours. We have two species here, the Three-spined and Ten-spined, both of which can be found in an amazing array of different habitats, from streams and ponds, to ditches and even mildly saline rock pools. The mating behaviour of the sticklebacks is one of the most fascinating of any animal; in the spring the males develop a rosy breast and blue eyes, and set about building a mound-shaped nest. Each entices as many females into his boudoir as he possibly can, then fertilizes the eggs. However, unlike many other fishy fathers, he doesn't then swim off into the sunset, but waits over his eggs, and even looks after the youngsters after they hatch out, protecting them against predators.

COMMON FROG

The dark mask worn by the Common Frog is one of the many ways you can tell them apart from our Common Toad. While it might not be entirely true to say that the Common Frog breathes through its skin, as most of its breathing is done the conventional way using mouth, nostrils and lungs, there is certainly a great deal of gas exchange through their amazing moist skin, which allows them to hibernate for several months under leaves and mud. Females are bigger than males, and they may live as long as eight years. I'd really recommend keeping some spawn from these remarkable and charming creatures to adult stage, so you can learn about their behaviour and development.

▲ *The masked bandit. Common Frogs are a key part of a pond ecosystem and sign of its health.*

GREAT CRESTED NEWT

This is our largest and rarest newt, and is afforded much needed protection by law, so it is illegal to handle, catch or harm these newts in any way. This is necessary, as habitat loss has led to the Great Crested Newt becoming increasingly rare throughout the UK, and once you see one, you'll understand why we'd want to protect them! During the day, these newts spend most of their time hiding on land (one reason why a log pile or wild part of your garden is essential if you've got a wild pond), but at night they come alive, and are voracious hunters. The crested part of the name refers to a jagged ridge that runs down the male's tail, which becomes more pronounced during breeding times.

AND THE ITTY BITTY STUFF!

These are all creatures for which you'll need a hand lens, a magnifying glass, or even better a microscope to get a look at, but it's well worth it. This could be your first look into a fascinating microscopic world!

OSTRACOD These crustaceans are often found browsing on aquatic leaves or mud. The body is enclosed in a bean-shaped shell, divided in two a bit like a mussel, but you may be able to discern the antenna and limbs protruding. Related to shrimps and crabs, as well as the

Daphnia and Cyclops listed below, ostracods swim by sweeping their antenna back and forth. Their protective shells are so effective that they fossilize well, and layers of earth that was once seabed can be dated through analysing their fossilized remains.

DAPHNIA Also known as water fleas, these are very common freshwater plankton, although you'll also find them amongst organic matter and even sold in pet shops as living fish food. It's great looking at these under a microscope, as they're transparent so you can see the moving limbs, compound eye and beating heart.

CYCLOPS Another planktonic organism, which is easy to see. Its name has obvious origins, the single large eye is quite obvious. Cyclops can be quite brightly coloured, although are more often a drab brown colour, and females are often seen carrying egg sacs.

▲ The Daphnia is a super-common kind of plankton, and food for many pond predators.

HELIOZA A wonderful and bizarre single-celled organism that you won't be able to see unless you have a decent microscope to hand, but it's well worth making the effort. Each is an amazing little miracle, like a little sun, with hair-like filaments bristling from the circular mid section.

HYDRA These are found attached to surfaces like floating leaves and the stems of plants in the water. Though a Hydra looks like a plant itself, it is actually an animal, usually green or pale brown, which uses stinging cells in its tentacles to sting and catch tiny floating prey. One of the most fascinating things about Hydra is that they can reproduce by separating a chunk off their body, which then grows into another individual.

Amazing aquatic larvae

BLOODWORMS

These tiny wriggling larvae are like threads of red cotton, smaller than you might be looking for in your net. They're the young of midges, which are like little mosquitoes, and like all the larvae here, are nothing like the adults at all. Once you've caught bloodworms (there are often hundreds of them in the muck and slime at the bottom of a pond, where they feed on old bits of animals and plants), watch the way they move, curling their body in a curious figure of eight movement. When they're ready to pupate, they rise to the surface, and the adults will emerge and fly away – if they can avoid becoming lunch for a hungry fish!

DRAGONFLY

If the adult is the fighter bomber of the pond above the surface, the dragonfly nymph is the Great White Shark of the

pond below it. These extraordinary aliens have a sort of mask-like lower jaw they can fire out to capture prey like tadpoles, and can shoot themselves around the pond by squirting water out of their bottoms. They are high-powered hunters, and if you do have one in your pond, make sure there's plenty for them to eat, or they'll munch *everything*! They emerge as adults in the same way as mayflies and damselflies, and if you wander around a pondside in the summer, you may well find their empty shells (known as exuvia or 'shucks') left behind on reed stems.

DAMSELFLY As adults it's easy to tell damselflies and dragonflies apart. Think of a fairytale scene: there's a damsel at the window of her castle fluttering her hanky in the breeze, and a great big horrible dragon coming to eat her. Damselflies are like her hanky; dainty, slender, gentle in flight (if not in deed). Dragonflies are just monsters, aggressive, bulky, possibly the most ferocious creatures in the world in comparison to their body size. This difference is also present in the nymphs, with damselfly nymphs also being much more delicate and taking smaller prey than dragonfly nymphs. Young damsels also have three prominent paddles at the rear end, which aid in getting around, and may spend as much as five years underwater getting fat, before clambering up a stem to the open air, splitting open their casing and emerging as a wondrous winged adult.

MAYFLY Though mayflies are most obvious when they emerge as fluttering adults, it's as nymphs that they really get their living done. Their lives as adults are legendarily short – most of them living no more than a day – and they don't even stop to feed, but just get on with making more mayflies. However, they have about two years as larvae beneath the surface of the water, feeding on algae and plants. You can tell the nymphs apart from other aquatic creatures by the two or three long, fine filaments like fragile threads sticking out of their back end.

Unlike the other larvae mentioned here, the Great Diving Beetle spends the majority of its adult life in the water too. However, it is a good flier when adult, and may be one of the first creatures to colonize a new pond. If you were a small frog or newt tadpole, this beast would be your worst nightmare, and probably the last thing you would ever see. As larvae, Great Diving Beetles are identified by huge sickle-shaped jaws, which they jab into prey, before injecting a digestive toxin into the prey and then sucking up the meat like a soup. Mmmmm, yummy! One of the coolest aspects of the larva is that it can stick its rear end up to the surface and actually breathe oxygen through a spiracle (breathing hole) at the end of its abdomen.

Making wildlife water features

Probably the most rewarding addition to a garden if you want to attract wildlife is a pond, but the best way of finding out about the creatures that might make their home there is to create a sort of fake pond – a wildlife water feature. The best thing to do would be to go to a car boot sale, or get on Ebay and try and get yourself an old (but still watertight) fish tank. Once the tank has been filled with fresh rainwater (tap water is not good for aquatic animals) all you need to do now is leave it outside and let nature take its course. First of all water boatmen, pond skaters and other winged water beasts will arrive, but if you were to leave it for months and even years, eventually you would end up with a fully functioning ecosystem there. I'm guessing, though, that you'll not be wanting to wait that long for your pond to get interesting, so this is a time to go out pond dipping. Get yourself a bucket and go and ferret around in several different waterways, and bring back some water wildlife to stock your pond.

A couple of things worth thinking about are oxygenation and food. A small area of water will soon go stagnant, and while this won't deter everything, adding an aeration device (bought cheaply from your local pet or aquarium shop) will certainly help life to thrive. Also, the critters you're bound to want in your pond are often predators, and will need live prey to feed on. You can buy water fleas from aquarium shops, but might as well fish for them yourself with your net! Make sure to top up the levels of tiny prey items regularly if you have a lot of predators like dragonfly larvae and sticklebacks in your tank.

It's essential to have a bank made of pebbles or gravel, so that amphibians can exit the water, and also aquatic plants with stems that leave the water, so larvae have somewhere to climb up and emerge as adults. This is one of the great highlights of the wildlife water feature. Directly after they emerge as adults, dragonflies and damselflies need to allow their wings to dry, and then additional time to pump blood into their wings. This is the one time you stand any chance of getting really close one of these flighty creatures.

A more permanent addition to the garden is an actual wildlife pond. In the past, ponds were set up for ornamental fish, and the presence of various wild creatures was more of an accident, but now more and more people are building ponds in their back garden with the hope of attracting newts and frogs, and also for the joy of seeing birds splashing about and enjoying a cooling bath.

Things to remember when making a wildlife pond are that many creatures within the pond will need to get in and out safely. A shallow area of water leading to a sloping bank will allow birds to bathe and drink there, and will also allow amphibians to crawl out of the pond once it's time for them to disperse. You need to be sure to have a wild section of your garden, perhaps with a woodpile and some wild plants, in order for wandering amphibians to make a home.

Snorkelling in lakes and rivers

In my local waterways the fauna has grown used to avoiding rowers and pleasure boaters, but has so little experience of snorkellers that it will let me get crazy close – I've had a Moorhen dragging nesting material right over the top of my head, and got closer to glorious, golden eyed Tufted Ducks than ever before.

Stick to small rivers, where you won't go out of your depth. Large, deep rivers, especially when swollen with floodwater, can be extremely dangerous. Other things to be wary of when snorkelling in freshwater environments are currents, cold and tangle hazards. The latter can be avoided by taking great care when snorkelling around areas of dense aquatic reeds, and in extreme cases carrying a diver's knife to possibly cut yourself free (also a necessity if diving or snorkelling anywhere there may be a risk of entanglement in rope or netting). Cold is obviously negated with a wetsuit, and currents by pure common sense!

Too often people dismiss the creatures that inhabit our freshwater environments, and don't think of taking the mask and snorkel with them when they're heading to the local river or lake. I've come face to face with a Pike in the reeds at a lake where my parents used to take us, and it was pretty impressive, I can tell you! On a smaller scale though, Sticklebacks are some of the most striking and fascinating living things in our nation – particularly the males when they're wearing their bright red breeding finery. It's also possible to see loads of crazy invertebrate life making its home in aquatic mud and plants.

Freshwater fish

We have about 50 species of fish living in Britain's freshwater environments, which anglers divide into four broad groups. Most numerous are probably the carp relatives (including Chub, Barbel, Tench, Roach and Dace), which are usually not predators, have rows of bony teeth and are comfy in slow or still waters. Fish of the salmon family (trout, salmon and Grayling) like cool, well-oxygenated water, and may undergo long migrations. Full on predators like Pike, Perch and Zander feed on other fish and have teeth to match, and then there's the smaller minnow-type fish like Sticklebacks, Bullhead and Stone Loach. All British fish lay eggs; none give birth to live young. The eggs are laid on the bottom or on plants, and then the male will spray his sperm or milt over the top of the eggs to fertilize them.

PIKE

This big fish has an even bigger presence in British folklore; stories tell of them seizing drinking cows by the lips and dragging them into the river! However with a large female only weighing in at 25 kg, it seems unlikely any Pike could conquer a cow... what they are much more likely to feed on are frogs, small mammals, ducklings and other fish, which makes them awesome predators all the same. Despite this reputation, the Pike is also known for its beautiful courtship ballet, with the smaller males chasing in packs after one huge female, nuzzling her tenderly, ascending to the surface together then dropping back down to the depths as if synchronized swimming. The best place to see Pike is in Stoney Cove in Leicestershire, where one corner of the quarry provides an almost 100 per cent chance of seeing these wondrous water wolves in their natural environment.

▲ The shark of the lake and river, Pike is a savage predator.

DACE

The slim and silvery Dace is a small fish, only rarely growing to the length of a standard ruler (30 cm), but nevertheless has been reported as living to 16 years old! Dace prefer the upper reaches of rivers, with cool, clear waters flowing over a gravelly bottom, and can be seen swimming near the surface in large numbers. They feed on insects, snails and plant matter.

CHUB

This is a much more thickset fish, with brandy-coloured flanks and pinkish fins. Another long-lived fish, some of the biggest specimens exceed 20 years in age. Chub are said to eat just about anything they can fit in their gobs, but will mostly eat zooplankton, freshwater crustaceans, insect larvae and very small fish.

SALMON

The well-known salmon runs of North America and the wildlife spectacles that ensue thereafter are perhaps one of the world's wildlife highlights. Few people realize that some of that wonder can be experienced here in the UK. Atlantic Salmon spend almost their entire lives at sea, but return to freshwater to spawn, swimming upriver to the places they were born in order to lay their eggs.

TROUT

The Brown Trout is our native species, whereas Rainbow Trout were introduced here from their native North America; both are prized food and game fish. You'll have no problems telling the two apart – one is brown; the other has rainbow stripes! Both are predators, feeding on insects, other fish, even small mammals. It takes three years for trout to mature and be able to breed. The Salmon family can be told apart from our other fish by their 'adipose fin', a small extra fin between the dorsal and tail fins.

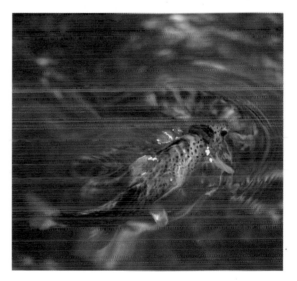

PERCH

These are very distinctive fish, with broad, black vertical stripes on a greenish body, and reddish fins. They'll shoal when they're small, but are loners when larger, and are full-on predators feeding on all sorts of invertebrates, crustaceans and fish larvae. They have sharp spines and gill covers, which can easily draw blood if they're handled; not to mention those vicious teeth.

Frogwatchin'

Throughout the world there are few more delightful or more threatened animals than the amphibians. Their remarkable moist skin, which allows gas and fluids to be taken straight into the body, makes them especially vulnerable to pollutants in the environment, and also a nasty fungus which kills amphibians is coursing around the world. With this in mind, we should all be trying to do whatever we can to inspire an interest in this wonderful animal group, and one of the best ways of doing this is to observe them going through their remarkable development to adulthood.

You will need a tank; preferably glass-sided so you can see what's going on inside without just looking down into it, and also a bucket to gather the spawn. Take care when gathering the spawn not to disturb mating pairs of frogs and toads, use a net rather than your hands, and try not to break the clumps of spawn apart. Fill the bucket with water and pond weed from the same pond as you take the spawn; you'll need a good supply of this pondweed for the tadpoles to feed on once they hatch out.

Gently pour the water, pondweed and spawn into the tank. Now, all you have to do is wait. The time it takes for them to develop is dependant on temperature, and if the tank is kept in the warmer environment in your house this should happen quicker than outside. Eventually, the tadpoles will start to hatch out, and the wonderful spectacle of their development begins.

In the first few days, they don't feed, clinging still to the jelly of their spawn or to a plant whilst nourishing themselves from their egg sac. After a few more days, the eyes and mouth will develop and start to open, and the tadpoles will start swimming about a bit. They'll start to feed on algae that's growing on the pondweed in the tank. Soon, feathery gills will be visible, which the tadpoles use to obtain oxygen from the water as fish do. These, however, will atrophy and eventually disappear as the tadpole moves towards an amphibious life spent both in and out of water.

The next stage is the back legs starting to develop. At this stage, the tadpoles start to become carnivorous, and will need some form of prey in the pond to keep them happy. A little very finely chopped meat or fish food should work. Alternatively just keep refreshing the tank water with water from the pond, and microorganisms and algae in the water will serve as food.

Finally the tail begins to shrink, the gills fade away as lungs are growing inside, and the tadpoles may come to the surface to gulp air. The front legs will start to come through, and now you need to be thinking about what to do with the froglets – once they're ready to leave the tank you really need to release them back into a pond, where they have a way of getting in and out of the water. As 99 per cent of tadpoles are lost in the wild due to natural pressures such as predation, lack of food and so on, your charges will be a valuable addition to the wild amphibians in your garden.

Riverside tracks and scat

The soft muddy ground alongside a water course can be the very best of substrate for you to locate tracks, and the added fact that so many animals come down to water to drink can make this the best of environments for wildlife detective work.

AMERICAN MINK

This predator is not a native of the UK, but has certainly set about making our waterways its own, after large numbers were released from fur farms by well-meaning animal rights activists. The American Mink has become the biggest threat in the UK to the Water Vole. Look for a five-toed track, with the little inside toe sometimes not registering, but the webbing between the toes often visible. Mink are about the size of domestic cats, so a stride length of 35cm is average – bigger than a stoat but much smaller than an otter. The scat is very oily, and consists of long black or brown slender cords which may fold back on themselves, and has hair, feathers or the remains of fish in it. They may leave these droppings on logs exposed at the water's edge as a way of scent marking, and can produce a very strong musky substance from their anal glands. Worth mentioning here is that without any sense of scale they can be difficult to tell apart from otters, but when seen in the flesh they are much smaller with darker fur, and have more weasely pointed faces.

WATER VOLE

This vole is the real victim of the release of American Mink into its environment, and is fast becoming quite a rare sight in the UK. The front and rear prints are quite different, with the front track showing four toes, and the rear showing five. They usually have a trotting gait, and leave oval scat in latrines that may contain thousands of pellets.

WATER SHREW

Britain's only venomous mammal, the Water Shrew is a fearsome little beastie, but you'll be surprised at quite how small it is (even though larger than our Common Shrew). There are five toe prints visible on both front and back prints, and they make a sort of hopping stride. The scat is a flattened pellet with tapered ends, and they may leave little piles of discarded chunks of prey items; usually invertebrates they've caught underwater.

FALLOW DEER

Introduced by the Normans for hunting, this beautiful deer has spread through much of Britain. The track is heart-shaped and cloven, and the scat is a fat pellet that falls apart as it dries out. The buck's flattened antlers are dropped in the autumn after the rut and may be found, but the blood-rich velvet that protects the antler early in the year is usually eaten by smaller animals as it has a high nutritional content.

GRASS SNAKE

Grass Snakes are surprisingly adept swimmers and are never found far away from freshwater sources, preying mainly on frogs. Though the movement trails of snakes may occasionally be discerned, a far more decisive proof of their presence is found in their shed (or sloughed) skins, which are transparent, but patterned with scale shapes. Unlike lizards, which shed their skins in chunks, snakes roll the whole lot off in one go, almost like they've taken off a sock.

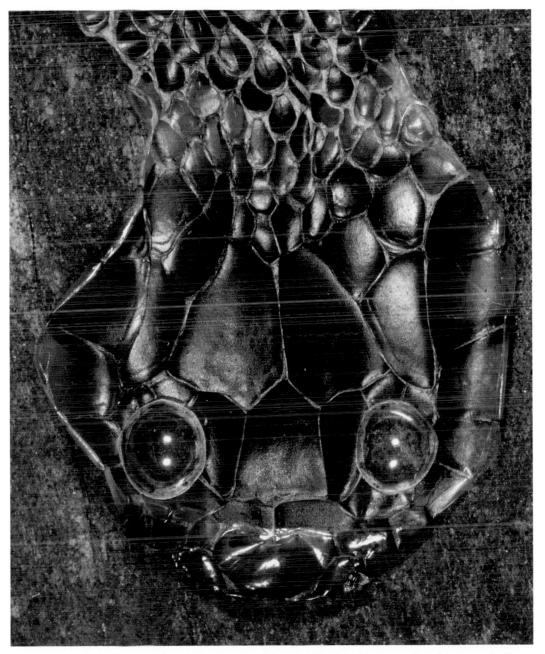

▲ Sloughed snake skins near to water are most likely to belong to a strong-swimming Grass Snake.

Canyoning

Canyoning is kind of the freshwater version of coasteering, a way of getting down steep and challenging water courses by whatever means necessary. The amount of kit needed is minimal, but the experience and common sense required is far more important. Flash floods may be rare on British rivers, but the kinds of environments where canyoning is popular are much more subject to such events. Checking weather reports therefore is essential, and prior planning should never be shortcut. My mind wanders back to a few years back when I decided to run a Welsh whitewater river without properly scoping the terrain. I got carried away with an exhilarating descent, and then all of sudden found myself stuck at the bottom of one waterfall, and at the top of another massive fall that was impossible to descend. I was trapped! Luckily I had a phone in a waterproof bag, and managed to call a friend who arrived with a rope to haul me out, but it might not have ended so happily – and I was hypothermic by the time they arrived. As always, I hope that I have learned the hard way, so you don't have to!

The most exciting rivers for canyoning have deep pools you can jump into, minor rapids that can be swum through, waterfalls to jump off or climb up, and sections of river that can be swum. Numerous outdoors companies offer organized canyoning trips, and seeking out one of those is the best way to get to grips with this exciting sport – going it alone is far too risky.

Basic equipment needed for canyoning is some clothing to keep you warm – Britain's freshwater environments are never warm, and the rivers of Scotland are icy cold even in mid summer. A thin wetsuit that you can still swim and move well in is a good idea, and many would use an oversuit in order to protect this wetsuit. Buoyancy or flotation devices are sensible, as is a helmet. If there are going to be long stretches when you may be floating or swimming downstream, an additional buoyant device such as an inflated inner tube can make a world of difference. While on the subject, one of the most fun canyoneering type events run regularly in the UK is the Glen Nevis river race, run by the Lochaber Mountain Rescue. Competitors travel down through Glen Nevis's many falls and rapids, using an inflatable of some kind to aid them.

Caving

If there's one adventure activity that really gives me the willies, it's caving. The first few times underground was no bother at all, but gradually as my caving experiences have got harder and harder, I've found myself getting more and more claustrophobic. This became a real issue after a challenge in a Welsh cave, aptly called 'The Long Crawl'.

This is basically a tube little wider than my waist, as long as a football pitch, which takes hours to pass through. For the entire

▲ *I may be smiling here, but caving really gives me heebie jeebies!*

distance it was like trying to crawl through the inside of a car tyre on your belly, and it just went on and on. So, now that I am thoroughly terrified of caves, I may not be the best person to try and convince you to give it a go...

It is, however, an environment worth exploring at some stage. Whilst above ground our nation was fully explored hundreds of years ago, underground new discoveries are made every year. The largest cave in the UK – Titan in Derbyshire – was only discovered a few years ago, underneath a farmer's field in the Peak District, and it is AWESOME!

In the tropics, caves are home to a huge variety of life, but here in the UK they can be quite sterile places, with the majority of animals found within the first 50 m or so. Bats are an obvious wildlife highlight; Lesser Horseshoe Bats particularly choose to roost in cave systems and coming out at night to go looking for insects. An invertebrate that chooses to hunt within caves is the Cave Spider, a good-sized arachnid that leaves its egg sacs hanging from the roof of the cave by silken threads. I've also found gammerus shrimps, fish, and even some rather surprised-looking frogs deep inside caves, washed in by flood waters.

Caving, spelunking, potholing or speleology should always be undertaken with knowledgeable professionals. Firstly the dangers of getting lost or hurt are quite high, secondly rescues are always horrendous, and lastly, weather conditions can make a massive difference to conditions inside a cave. In 2008, two cavers were killed in one of the most popular and apparently easy cave systems in the UK, when high rainfall combined with icy ground conditions to create a deadly flashflood.

Though not all caves contain rivers, all the caves in the UK were formed by the action of freshwater; eroding solid rock and reacting chemically with limestone to create dissolving acid, and that is why caves are included in this chapter. Naturally, it is the areas of hard limestone rock that have the most extensive cave systems. Derbyshire and Yorkshire, southern Wales, Northern Ireland and the Mendips are some of the hotspots for those crazy caving dudes. A few terms you may need to know: a *squeeze* is a narrow gap that requires the caver to compress their body to get through; a *pitch* is a section of vertical cave that needs to be climbed or abseiled down with the aid of ropes and or ladders; a *sump* is a section of cave that has filled with water, and you may need to freedive or even use tailored scuba-diving gear to get through it.

Five freshwater birds

DIPPER

The ultimate exponent of the rushing watercourse, with its dumpy dark-coloured body, and its habit of occasionally cocking its short tail upwards, you could possibly mistake the Dipper for a Wren… until it plunges straight into fast-flowing water, to hunt for aquatic insects or shrimps. The white breast is a bit of a giveaway too. Dippers may actually build their nests behind raging waterfalls, providing great protection from predators. You're most likely to see one hopping from rock to rock, before ducking into the water and emerging with a bug in its bill.

KINGFISHER

KINGFISHER While the Dipper is the master in whitewater, in more slow-moving waters there is only one king amongst the fishers. This must be one of the most distinctive and most loved of our small birds, and for good reason; nothing brightens a riverside walk quite so much as the flash of electric blue as a Kingfisher zips past. If you want to increase your chances of seeing a Kingfisher feeding, wait by a bare branch overhanging the water in a place that they are known to frequent. If you're lucky, a bird may perch there and cast its remarkable eyesight into the river in search of a fish. Check the lower mandible of the bill – if it's orange you're looking at a female or a juvenile, dark and it's an adult male. The nest is a burrow, dug out in the riverbank by both birds.

TEAL The Teal is ever such a pretty little duck, and I say little because it's our smallest duck. Although we do have resident birds, their numbers are greatly increased by winter visitors. The males are much more dramatic than the females, with their chestnut-orange head, and an English racing green stripe through the eye. Both sexes, however, have a green speculum – that's a brightly coloured wing panel that's clearly visible when the wings are folded. Teal are well known for their great ability to take off almost vertically when they're startled, their small size making them agile flyers.

CORMORANT It may seem weird to include a bird here that is so closely affiliated with the sea, but the fact is Cormorants are very adaptable birds, and are increasingly found around rivers, lakes and ponds. I've even sat and watched a pair fishing in a grotty canal in the East End of London – and doing surprisingly well! It feeds by

swimming at the surface, then diving down and swimming beneath the water until it can catch a fish. This immersion does create great demands on the Cormorant however. Its feathers are less water-repellent than a duck's, and it does not coat them with oils to repel water. Thus, you'll often see a Cormorant standing out of the water with its wings spread, using the sun and wind to dry off the feathers. Without this behaviour, they would find flying with waterlogged feathers very hard indeed.

WHOOPER SWAN

The Whooper is a winter visitor that remains faithful to certain favoured sites, migrating into north and central regions from Iceland when their preferred food of grasses and grains becomes unavailable. The Whooper (in the front of the picture) is larger and longer-necked than Bewick's Swan (behind), and the bill is distinctive, with a large triangular patch of yellow on a black background. Bewick's has a much smaller blob of yellow on the bill, and lacks the boisterous honking call of the Whooper (which sounds like Mr Toad's car horn!).

Lighting a fire

Fire has been marked out as one of the first technological advances to set us apart from animals. Fire offers warmth, it keeps away bugs, its heat can turn inedible food into dinner and it can provide a means of signalling for help. It is the most important tool an outdoors specialist can have in the event of an emergency, but it must be treated with great respect. When the environment is very dry, a carelessly lit fire can cause unimaginable damage. Accelerants like petrol and alcohol must be used with great care – many people have been disfigured by a fire exploding or raging out of control. In fact, just a little splash of insect repellent may be enough to get it started. Unless you have the land-owner's permission, only start a fire in the countryside in genuine emergency situations, never start fires in hot, dry conditions or in high-risk environments such as heathland and peaty moorland, and monitor your fire with very close care.

You may think of fire as being an easy part of the survival equation, but I can ensure you this is not the case; I've torn my hair out with fury whilst attempting and failing to light a fire countless times. Practise learning to get a fire going in a safe, approved environment; it's a skill that could save your life one day.

GETTING STARTED

The three essential ingredients for a raging fire are air, fuel, and heat. Lose any one of these, and your fire will go out. Make sure you have a well-ventilated site for your fire; digging a small trench under your fire – or two in the shape of a cross – can help air to circulate. It is also important to think about where the smoke is going to go – if you are sleeping in a small cave with no airflow, it'll be really uncomfortable if you build the fire right inside. The flip side of this is that the fire has to be protected from strong winds, which will put it out.

Fuel can be broken down into three elements. Tinder is very dry, fine material that can be lit with a spark. Paper, dried grasses, cotton fluff, downy feathers or the insides of old bird's nests, chunks of dried tree resin, wood shavings, ground-up dry fungus, birch bark, dead pine needles, straw – these all make good tinder. However, on a wet day, you can have all the potential tinder you could ask for, and trust me, you'll still struggle.

Kindling is the material you need to take a small flame into a viable fire. Small twigs, twisted up balls or rings of paper, dry pine cones, bark, rags, dry rotten wood, leaves, thick cardboard – all of these will get your fire going. Then you can increase the size of the fuel until you work your way up to harder, longer lasting fuels such as heavy dead wood, split green wood, dried animal dung, animal fats or coal.

Gather all these materials before starting (you don't want to be going off searching for the next twig just as your fire gets going), and clear a space where you can contain your fire. This may be as simple as clearing away leaves to reveal the soil, or encircling a hearth with rocks. Make sure not to take porous rocks or ones that have been submerged in water – as the water within them expands with heat, they may explode. If building a fire on snow, make a fireplace out of green logs. In windy conditions it may help to dig a hole or trench and sink the fire into it.

GETTING IT GOING

There are several different ways of building and starting a fire, but the one I learnt in Scouts and have used ever since is the tepee. First you need to make a small pile of tinder, and then stack a tepee of your smallest, best quality kindling over the top of it. In an ideal world, you then apply a flame to the tinder in several places, and it all gets going. Blowing gently on the lit tinder will help getting it going, or if you have a good breeze, light on the upwind side. Matches are great as long as you can keep them *and* the striker dry, lighters are perfect until they break, using a lens (from your camera, magnifying glass or binoculars) to focus the sun's rays onto tinder works remarkably well, and various survival matches (such as metal matches, flint and steel) are worth having in your survival kit.

FIRE WITHOUT MATCHES

I've made fire many times with primitive methods, but I've probably given up more times! It takes a huge amount of time, effort and frustration, but it is a great skill to have, and worth learning and practising.

The fire plough uses friction to make a spark. You need a chunk of softwood, a stick of hardwood, and some excellent tinder. Use the stick to create a long groove in the softer log and place some tinder at the end of it. Then push the end of the stick repeatedly through the groove up and down, up and down. This will grind out wood dust, which will be heated by friction, and hopefully get the tinder going. An alternative is the hand drill, where you drill the point of the hardwoood stick into the soft wood with your hands, or a makeshift bow. You rub your hands together causing the stick to rotate as quickly as possible.

▲ *The teepee method of setting a fire.*

▲ *Dry tinder and wood make fire lighting seem quite easy... it's a different story in the wet!*

▲ *You don't want to be trying this for the first time in winter drizzle!*

Free freshwater grub

Reedmace is found at the riverside, it's the plant that's sometimes called Cat's Tail or Bulrush. It's not the familiar furry bits that you want, but the rhizomes (plump underground stems) found deep under the water. Chuck these into the fire until the outer spongy stem has blackened, then suck the starch out of the fleshy centre. The best time to collect the rhizomes is in winter, as that's when their starch content is highest.

As a youngster, I was a bit obsessed with my SAS handbook, and took its advice to make a soup out of Stinging Nettles, which are found all over the place. They're high in vitamins C and D, and cooking them renders the stings useless. So I boiled up a whole bunch in the woods, and felt like Robinson Crusoe! However, they were pretty stringy, and there is always the problem of what you do if you're stranded and you haven't got a nice pot to boil them in. Turns out they're just as good (if that's the right word) if you just wilt them in the heat above your fire. Don't expect to be taking them home to accompany your Sunday roast though...

One of the finest free foods to be found in the wilds is freshwater crayfish, and if you fish for them right, you may actually be doing the environment a service. Our own British White-clawed Crayfish is too small to make a decent meal, and is quite scarce. However, its place has been all but taken over by the American Signal Crayfish. This intruder was brought into the country to be a food source, but escaped its boundaries, and is much larger and hardier than our native species, so has pushed it out. And as if this wasn't enough to teach people a lesson about introducing non-native species, a new even larger species (the Marbled Crayfish) is

▲ Eat an introduced crayfish and you'll get a good meal and do the environment a favour!

now making an appearance in Britain. As crayfish can cross large areas of dry land, it is only a matter of time before this beast is also running amok through our rivers. Our native White-clawed Crayfish gets its name from the white underside of its pincers, whereas the Signal Crayfish has obvious signal red pincers and is a good deal larger; so will make a better meal.

Catching crayfish is not a labour-intensive way of finding food – you can use a trap that can be left in the river while you do other things. Perhaps the best trap is made from a large soft drinks bottle (as seen in the photo). Cut off the top of the bottle about a quarter-way down, put in some bait, and add some stones to weight it down. Anything smelly that will dissipate into the water a bit will work really well as bait: fish paste, rotting fish, anything a bit mushy and stinky. Put the top of the bottle back in so the top is pointing down towards the base. Next, fix the top into place, and drop the bottle into the water. Leave it overnight, and the crayfish should swim inside to investigate the bait, but then be unable to leave.

KEEPING RECORDS

You don't need to be great with pen or brush to make a worthwhile record of your wildlife encounters in words and pictures. Even if you're not so interested in identification, your notebook, photo, or film will be a permanent memento of your adventures, to be enjoyed over the years to come.

Records and reminders

If my house was on fire and there was only time to rescue one thing, I'd bypass my telly, and head straight for my collection of photos and my old battered diaries. Memories are so precious to us as humans, irreplaceable mementos of perfect moments and times past, priceless records of experiences that might otherwise be lost to the eroding tides of time. And they're not only precious to us; many modern scientific trends in nature have been deduced from the observations and records of amateur naturalists, who've noted things such as the springtime arrival of certain birds and butterflies over many years.

If you want to identify animals and plants, you'll find taking field notes and making sketches is as helpful as taking photos, sometimes more so. You can use one notebook for notes and sketches, or carry a ruled pad for the former and a plain one for the latter if you prefer – although when you're working fast to record details about an unfamiliar animal, you'll probably find it helpful to keep notes and sketches in the same place.

WHAT TO WRITE

This is really up to you. Basics like date, time of day and weather conditions help to set the scene. If you're trying something new, such as moth-trapping for the first time, noting down exactly what you did can help you refine your technique and get better results in the future. If you want to take field notes of an animal or plant you don't recognise, the more detail you can record on the spot, the better. Try to note down your impressions of colours, patterns, shapes and proportions. For animals, try to record the way they move, any sound they make and any striking behaviour. For plants, pay as much attention to leaves and stems as to flowers, and note the way the parts are arranged on the plant (e.g. leaves in pairs or alternate, flowers in a cluster or single). It's often useful to draw comparisons with more familiar species – if the way it flies reminds you of a Swift, or the way its foliage hangs down reminds you of a willow tree, say so.

WHAT TO DRAW

Don't let insecurities about your artistic talents put you off drawing wildlife. Field sketches don't have to be works of art to be valuable aids to identification, and besides, practice makes perfect. If you're drawing in a rush – say, a bird that may fly off any moment   forget about tricky aspects like getting the overall shape of the thing just right. Concentrate instead on noting the exact positions of any markings. You can draw these onto a simple, generic outline and make sure you describe the shape accurately in words. Using colour is fun (although you may not have time). Coloured pencils are probably the easiest media to use in the field.

Take some time to sketch animals and plants at your leisure. Not only is it a rewarding skill to acquire, it also helps focus the mind and compels you to really look carefully at them in detail, helping to build your familiarity and making future encounters all the more rewarding.

Using field guides

Field guides are there to help you identify what you see, and also to help you predict what you might see (and where and when). Identification isn't the be-all and end-all of enjoying wildlife, but a bit of background knowledge about the animal or plant you're looking at can really enhance your enjoyment of an encounter.

Using field guides is a bit of an art, especially when it comes to the large groups like birds or moths. When choosing one, make sure it covers the places you'll be doing most of your wildlife-watching but not too far beyond, make sure the illustrations are big and clear enough and I'd definitely recommend getting one with good-sized distribution maps. Any field guide that has extra 'keys' or guidance to help you work your way towards an identification is worth considering. You may not be able to take your field guide or guides everywhere with you – you'd need several books to comprehensively cover everything and other kit may have to take priority – but peruse the books when you're at home to help develop your familiarity with what you've seen or hope to see.

Taking photos

First off, your kit. You can take great photos with everything from a giant SLR (single lens reflex) camera right down to your mobile phone, and each has its own benefits and shortcomings. A mobile phone fits in your pocket, so when you see that peculiar caterpillar on the way to the shops you can get a shot of it. An SLR can fit a huge variety of lenses, so you can take macro shots of tiny insects that are right in front of you, or zoomed shots of birds half a mile away. The middle-ground option is a compact camera with a small zoom lens to give a bit of telephoto pulling power. However, whatever your weapon of choice, the principles for using light, framing a shot and giving an image 'life' are all the same.

LIGHT

I'll not bore you with F stop numbers here; those are topics for another tome. I just want to talk about using available light to the best advantage. A lot of that has to do with time of day. The magic hours of pre-dusk and early mornings will give you lovely rich light, while cloudy days and full-on noon sunshine can give you bleached out or flat-looking shots. Having the light behind you to illuminate your subject is the classic method, but great silhouette shots can be achieved shooting directly into the sun, particularly if you use your subject to mask the direct sunlight. Artificial light in the form of a flash can be vital – not just when working at night, but also when working in macro, or as a fill flash when wanting to take the edge off very contrasty shots. Flashes are great, but have obvious downfalls when using them to photograph wild animals – if the subject sees the flash go off it will probably make a run for it!

SHUTTER SPEED

How fast your shutter opens and closes defines the amount of time over which an image is being recorded. Faster shutter speeds (if there is sufficient light) give a crisper, static image of things that are moving, whereas slower shutter speeds may record some of that motion as blur. It's worth experimenting with this, as nothing gives an image more of an impression of movement than a little application of slow shutter speed. To get the feel of this, try taking shots from the window of a moving car; you'll get some wacky results! Another time slow shutter speeds work wonders is at night, shooting landscapes from a tripod. If

▲ The blur in this image gives a feeling of movement as the thrush smashes a snail shell.

you want to pick up the moon and the stars, simply set up a 20- or 30-second exposure – a little extra light will come out really powerfully. The flip side of all this stuff is that using fast shutter speeds can really give a sense of a moment caught in time, a running deer 'frozen' mid step, or an owl with its wings poised wide open whilst flying.

FRAMING

Start with a very conventional framing – treating the animal as if it were in a portrait, that is, slap bang in the middle of your shot. Try to avoid huge, blank areas of sky or ground. However, as your skills develop, these spaces become an integral part of your photo – suddenly the perched bird of prey is positioned to the corner of a photo, and the viewer follows its gaze to the expanse of farmland it will soon be hunting in. Try not to make your images too 'busy'. Simplicity is one of the chief elements of beauty. However, at the other extreme – if there are literally thousands of subjects – try to make them completely fill the frame with no end in sight, this gives the viewer a sense that the swarm of bees or flock of waders might actually go on forever... Try to get a moment

▲ Conventional portrait style framing can be very effective, as here with this Wood Mouse.

when an animal is looking right at the camera, and you can see the glint of light in their eyes. In other instances (particularly with birds) a profile is much more effective.

Making films

The principles for taking moving images of wildlife are very similar to those of still shots, but in order to make a great wildlife or adventure film, you will need to see beyond the shot, and start thinking about story. Shots of 15 different types of animals just sitting around won't make a film – you'll need to get shots of them exhibiting various behaviours, film them at different times of year, or film your own personal journey of discovery in finding them. Always have in your mind how a film might cut together; you'll need to go from a wide establishing shot, to something that shows your subject in more personal detail. Then perhaps cut to some close-ups, back to a wide shot, then a mid-range shot and so on. Be aware of what shots look good when they follow each other, and which jar terribly.

In order to give your film life, give it a voice. At the very least, put a voiceover on it after you've edited the footage together, but even better take a role in them yourself. I started off my filming career making totally self-shot films, but had to feature in them myself. I would turn the camera around in my hand using the flip out screen to see what I was filming, or put the camera on a tripod, putting myself into the world of the animals I was filming. One piece of advice my first ever boss gave me, was to never act like a presenter, but to just chat to the camera as if it were a mate down the pub. It's a far more inclusive way of talking, drawing the audience in, as if you're about to tell them some big secret... As I learnt my trade as a presenter and cameraman without anyone else around, it was much easier to get into the swing of this.

When you're self-shooting, it's essential to show that you are showing, making the device of shooting yourself totally visible. Leave in camera wobbles and focusing, and the bit where you turn the camera on and off. If I think the viewer still won't have got it, I'll get another camera and get a wide shot of me filming myself! This adds to the sensation that you are alone doing the job, and the corresponding roughness is understood by the viewer – without it, you'll be competing with the top end professional filmmakers in terms of quality, and not to put too fine a point on it – you'll lose.

Always think about storyline – think beginning, middle and end. Think about teasing the people who are watching with little titbits of information and images, rather than just giving everything to them on a plate. If you have footage of a Peregrine taking another bird out of the sky, tease it early in your film, then build up to the grand showing of the killer sequence later on. Think about giving a viewer reasons to stick with you.

Think about sound almost more than you think about pictures. Heavy wind noise on microphones renders sound worthless, but tiny elements of soundscape can bring a scene to life. One of my personal favourites is placing a mic down next to a trail of ants passing over a big leaf; the leaf acts like a drum and every one of their footsteps can be heard. Likewise, the dripping of water off leaves or from a stalactite in a cave – little sounds like this give more atmosphere than any line of voiceover commentary can.

▲ *Making your own wildlife films gives you the chance to get creative, and can be really rewarding.*

What to do with your records

This really is up to you. Maybe for you all the joy is in the actual making of notes or taking of images and once you have them you're quite happy for them to just gather dust (or metaphorical dust in the case of digital photos and recordings). If you do want to revisit those magic moments, there are all sorts of ways you can do this.

You can keep your notebooks as they are, or transfer notes to a pristine new book or file which lives at home and doesn't get bashed around in the field. This will also enable you to 'tidy up' the notes you made, and add relevant extras – you could turn your day's goose count or orchid list into a table or pie-chart if that's what you like to do.

The online equivalent of the notebook is the blog. You can set up free blogs at many websites now (try www.blogger.com), and the great advantage of these is that you can add your digital pics or video clips, as well as typing up your field notes and adding scans of your sketches. This also makes it really easy to share your experiences with friends, family and even complete strangers (remember to keep your personal details hidden when online). It's the perfect way of spreading a little wildlife joy into the lives of others and encouraging your nearest and dearest to join you in your fascinating hobby.

FINDING OUT MORE

FURTHER READING

If you've been inspired to start on your own adventures with wildlife, a bit of further reading will really add to your enjoyment next time you go out into the great outdoors. Here's a small selection of my favourite books for starters.

Allaby, Michael, *Oxford Companion to Zoology*, Oxford University Press, 1999. A dictionary of zoological terms, which I've found very useful over the years.

Attenborough, Sir David, *Life* series, BBC Books, various dates.
Life of Mammals, Life on Earth, Life in Cold Blood, Life in the Undergrowth, Life of Birds, The Private Life of Plants
I can't have a bibliography that doesn't mention the single biggest influence on natural history in the media ever, Sir David Attenborough. His books, like his films, are alive with humour, fascination and awe, and every word is worth reading. For a taste of Sir David's early life as an original adventure naturalist, look out for the *Zoo Quest* series of books and films, real seat of your pants stuff!

Baker, Nick, *New Amateur Naturalist* Collins, 2004. Along with the *First Time Naturalist*, and many of Nick's other books, this should be the first stop for any beginner planning on getting into biology and a life with wild animals. Inspired by Gerald Durrell's iconic *Amateur Naturalist*, my old sparring partner Nick shows you a zillion ways to study wildlife, at home and in the field.

Baker, Nick, *Nick Baker's Bug Book*, New Holland, 2002. I wish this book had been about when I was a nipper! With endless tips and information on the minibeasts that enter our world, and loads of tips for how to get an eye on theirs. A great starter on invertebrate life with much to interest children and adults alike, this is a must for every naturalist's bookshelf.

Buczacki, Stefan, *Fauna Brittanica*, Hamlyn, 2002. A strange mix of good solid natural history, myths and legends, folklore and fancy, this book is almost an almanac of the British countryside; good fun to dip in and out of.

Byatt, Andrew, Alastair Fothergill and Martha Holmes, *The Blue Planet: A Natural History of the Oceans*, BBC Books, 2001. From a team at the BBC's famed Natural History Unit, this companion to the TV series will open your eyes to the hidden wonders of the world's oceans.

Cliff, Peter *Mountain Navigation*, Max Design, 2006. If you want to learn about navigation, buy this book. It's cheap, it's easy to understand, it's flawless. Get it!

Couzens, Dominic, *The Secret Lives of Garden Birds*, Christopher Helm, 2002. Couzens does more than just watch birds; he lives their lives, understands them, really gets beneath the feathers and gives individual species personalities. There is a lifetime of understanding in here, and it's packed with the basic poetry of nature.

Flannery, Tim, *Throwim Way Leg*, Atlantic Press, 1998. Flannery is probably the closest living thing to Wallace: adventurer, anthropologist, biologist. A great yarn and some amazing critters!

Fothergill, Alastair, *Planet Earth: As You've Never Seen it Before*, BBC Books, 2006. Based on the wonderful BBC series, this is a truly inspiring look at our planet.

McGavin, George, *Field Guide to Insects and Spiders*, Dorling Kindersley, 2004. My old pal George writes some cracking books, and this is one of the most accessible and best laid-out of all invertebrate guides, with the tales of a lifetime of bug bothering experience behind them.

Mears, Ray and Gordon Hillman, *Wild Food*, BBC Books, 2007. I may dabble in the dark arts of wild food, but Ray Mears really is the master. Forget any other TV pretenders, what Ray doesn't know about foraging and feeding yourself from the land isn't worth knowing. This book gives a real insight into how our forebears may have used the food around them for sustenance.

Reynolds, Ross, *Philips Guide to the Weather*, Philips, 2000. A good scientific introduction to weather, though perhaps not as practical as one might need.

Sterry, Paul, *Collins Complete Guide to British Wildlife*, Collins, 1997. The perfect companion for a day out in the countryside. Whether you need to differentiate between a Silver-washed or High Brown Fritillary, or tell a Bloody-nosed Beetle from a Cockchafer, this is the perfect place to start!

Wallace, Alfred Russell, *Malay Archipelago*, Periplus, 2000 (originally published in 1869). The best adventure tale of all time, and all the better because it's true. Wallace travelled through areas of Asia that even today are remote and wild, and tells tales of pet orang-utans, cannibals and endless new scientific discoveries. Required reading for every adventure naturalist.

Walters, Martin, *Gardens For Wildlife*, Aura Books, 2007. A good little book about getting a garden that can attract and keep happy a whole range of wildlife.

Wiseman, Lofty, *SAS Survival Handbook*, Collins, 2009. First published 20 years ago, and recently updated, this was my constant companion as a kid. Endless info on how to stay alive in all kinds of sticky situations.

RECORDINGS OF BIRD SONGS
Sample, Geoff, *Collins Bird Songs and Calls of Britain and Northern Europe*, Collins, 1996. Though Geoff may be a little too softly spoken, I'm going to go out on a limb and say this is the best set of bird song CDs for Britain on the market. Download them onto your MP3 player and get learning.

iDentify Bird Songs, www.birdguides.com. These wonderful guides have revolutionized the way we can learn about wildlife. Upload them to your MP3 player and you can have a complete library of bird songs and calls in your pocket. A DVD version is available too, with footage of the birds in various situations, distribution maps and other great info. A great way to learn about the avian world.

Useful contacts

This is just a tiny taster of the many organizations that can help you find out more about wildlife and outdoor adventuring. Most of them would appreciate some help from you too! You can try your hand at all sorts of activities as a volunteer, take a course, go on an expedition, or just join some like-minded people for a day out. Check out the websites for ideas, but don't just read all about it, get involved!

BTCV
www2.btcv.org.uk

DUKE OF EDINBURGH'S AWARDS
www.dofe.org

FIELD STUDIES COUNCIL
www.field-studies-council.org

PLANTLIFE
www.plantlife.org.uk

PEOPLE'S TRUST FOR ENDANGERED SPECIES
http://ptes.org

SCOUT ASSOCIATION
www.scouts.org.uk

SURFERS AGAINST SEWAGE
www.sas.org.uk

SUSTRANS
www.sustrans.co.uk

TREES FOR LIFE
www.treesforlife.org.uk

THE WILDLIFE TRUSTS
www.wildlifetrusts.org

WILDFOWL AND WETLANDS TRUST
www.wwt.org.uk

Index

A-frame shelters 50
American Mink 136
American Signal Crayfish 144
anemones 72
Angel Shark 88
Angelfish 90
aquatic larvae 128-9
Atlantic Salmon 133
Attenborough, David 114
Autumn Lady's Tresses 60

Badger 116-17
Baker, Nick 35
Basking Shark 83
bats
    bat boxes 56
    weather sense 104
Bay of Fundy 74
Beadlet Anemone 72
bearings 102-3
Bee Orchid 59
Beech 33
bee boxes 43-6
Ben Nevis 101
Bewick Swan 141
binoculars 19
bird boxes 58
birdsong 28-30
blackberries 118
Blackbird 30
Blackcap 52
Blackthorn 58
Bladderwort 112
blogs 153
Bloodworm 128
Blue Shark 88
Bottlenose Dolphin 92
bouldering 106
Bramble 118
Brimstone Butterfly 45
Bristletail 86
Brown Hare 77
Brown Rat 55
Brown Trout 133
bubble rings 89
bug bothering 40-6
bug palaces 57-8
Butterfish 72
butterflies
    butterfly bar 46
    caterpillar catching 42
    forests 44-5
Butterwort 112

Cairngorms 115
cameras 22-3
canopy ropework 38
canyoning 138

Capercaillie 114
carnivorous plants 112-13
carp 132
caterpillar catching 42
Cave Spider 139
caving 139
Cep 62
cetaceans 92
Chaffinch 30
Chanterelle 62
chestnuts 33
Chicken of the Woods 63
Chub 133
clothing 17, 23
clouds 104-5
coasteering 85
cockles 94
Comma Moth 37, 45
Common Blue Butterfly 44
Common Buzzard 99, 110
Common Dolphin 92
Common Frog 126
Common Limpet 70
Common Sand Wasp 78
Common Seal 83
Common Shore Crab 73
Common Sun Star 91
Common Toad 126
compass 102-3
Conger Eel 88, 90
cooking 62-4, 94, 142-4
Cormorant 87, 141
Cornish Sucker 73
Crab Apple 118
crabs 70, 73
crayfish 144
crickets 104
Cuckoo 28
Curlew 75, 99
Cyclops 127

Dace 132
Daisy 118
Damselfly 128-9
Dandelion 118
Daphnia 127
Death Cap 63
deciduous trees 31
deer 53, 115, 116
    tracks and signs 54, 136
deodorant 17-18
dewclaws 116
Dipper 140
distance travelled 103
dolphins 92
Dotterel 114

downwind 18
Dragonfly 128
drawing 149
ducks 76, 86, 141
Dune Wolf Spider 78
Dunlin 75, 99
Dutch Elm disease 32

earwig home 43
edible plants 94, 118
eels 88, 90
Eider Duck 86
Elm 32
English Oak 33
Eskimo roll 81-2
evergreen trees 31

Fallow Deer 136
False Chanterelle 62
Feral Goat 117
field guides 22, 150
film making 152
fires 64, 142-3
fish
    freshwater 124, 132-3, 144
    rockpools 72-3
    sea fish 90-1
Five Finger Gully 101
Five-Spot Burnet 36
flash photography 150
flotsam and jetsam 77
Fly Agaric 63
Fly Orchid 59, 60
footprints 20
fossil hunting 93
freeclimbing 109
frogs 126, 134
Fulmar 86
fungi 62-3

Gannet 84
Gatekeeper Butterfly 45
geese 76
gleaners 75
Glyder mountains 102-3
goats 117
Golden Eagle 99, 111
Golden Plover 99
GPS 101, 102
Grass Snake 137
grasshoppers 104
Great Black-backed Gull 76
Great Crested Newt 126
Great Diving Beetle 129
Great Pond Snail 124
Great Skua 84
Great Tit 30

Grey Seal 84
Grey Squirrel 52, 55
Grizzly Bear 69
gulls 76

Hairy Porcelain Crab 73
hammocks 51
hand lenses 21
Harbour Porpoise 92
Harbour Seal 83
Hazel Dormouse 55
Hedgehog 57
Helioza 127
hibernaculum 112
Holly Blue Butterfly 44
honeydew 32
Hummingbird Hawkmoth 36
Hydra 127

insects, bug bothering tips 40-6

kayaking 80-2
kelp forests 90
Kingfisher 140
kit 21-3
knives 21
Knot 75

Lady's Slipper Orchid 59
Large White Butterfly 45
Lava Spire 75
Lavender 58
Lime 32
limpets 70, 94
Little Owl 56
Lizard Orchid 61
lizards 79
Lochaber Mountain Rescue 101

magnetic variation 102
Mako Shark 88
Malay Archipelago 11
maps 101-2
Marbel Crayfish 144
Marjoram 58
Mayfly 129
Mermaid's Purse 78
mice 53, 55
microscopes 22
Milk Parsley 44
mink 136
Minke Whale 92
Mistle Thrush 54
moth mix 35
moth traps 34
Mother of Pearl Moth 37

moths 34–7
    caterpillar catching 42
Mountain Ash 32
mountain biking 48–9
Muntjac Deer 54
mushrooms 62–3
mussels 94
mustelids 77

Natterjack Toad 77
nets 123
nettles 37, 144
newts 123, 126
Night-Scented Stock 58
Northern Nightingale 52
notebooks 22, 149

Oak 33
Oak Bush-cricket 31
Oddie, Bill 30
Orange Tip Butterfly 45
Orca 83
orchids 59–61
Ordnance Survey maps
    101–2
Ostracod 126–7
Otter 77, 87, 136
outdoor clothing 23
owls
    birdsong 28
    owl boxes 56–7
    signs 55

paddling 81
Peacock Butterfly 37, 45
Pearl-bordered Fritillary 45
Peppery Furrow 70
Perch 132, 133
Peregrine Falcon 111
pishing 28–9
photography 150–1
Pike 132
Pine Processionary Moth
    37
pitfall traps 40–1
Plover 70
pond dipping 123–9
pooter 41–2
Porbeagle Shark 88
porpoises 92
pots 21
prawns 94
Primrose 58
Ptarmigan 115
Pyramidal Orchid 61

Ragged Robin 58
Rainbow Trout 133
Ramshorn Snail 124
raspberries 118
rays 78
Razor Shell 79, 94

records 149–53
Red Admiral Butterfly 37
Red Deer 53, 116
Red Kite 110
Red Squirrel 52
Reed Mace 144
Reindeer 115
Ringed Plover 70
Robin 30
Rock Samphire 94
rockpools 70–3
Roe Deer 53
Rowan 32

salmon 132, 133
Samphire 94
Sand Lizard 79
Sanderling 75
Sandhopper 77
sandy shores 77–9
scallops 91
scat 18–20
scrambling 109
scuba diving 88
Sea Beet 94
sea birds 84, 86, 87
Sea Kale 94
sea kayaking 80–2
Sea Rocket 94
Sea Slater 77
seafood 94
Seagrass 90
seagulls 76
seahorses 90
seals 83, 84
sea squirts 90
Sessile Oak 33
Severn Bore 74
Shag 87
sharks 78, 83, 88
shellfish 70, 75, 79, 94
shelters 50–1
Shore Clingfish 73
Shrew 55
shrimp 94
sketching 149
slugs 42–3
Small Pearl-bordered
    Fritillary 45
Small Tortoiseshell Moth
    37, 45
snail stew 42–3
snails 124
Snakelocks Anemone 72
snakes 137
snorkelling
    freshwater 131
    sea 88
Song Thrush 54
spiders 78, 139
sport climbing 106
spotting scopes 19

squirrels 52, 55
Star Ascidian 72
starfish 91
stick shaking 40
Stickleback 124, 131
Stinging Nettle 144
Stoat 53, 136
storms 104, 105
strawberries 118
Strawberry Anemone 72
Sundew 113
survival kits 22
survival techniques 50–1
Swallowtail Butterfly 44
Swallowtailed Moth 36
swans 141
sweep netting 41
Sweet Chestnut 33
swish test 23
Sycamore 32
Sycamore Moth 31

tarpaulins 50
Tawny Owl
    birdsong 28
    owl boxes 56
    signs 55
Teal 141
telescopes 19
Thresher Shark 88
tides 69, 74
toads 77, 126
torches 18
tracking 20
tracks and signs
    coasts 76
    forests 54–5
    mountains 116–17
tree surgeons 38
trees 31–3
trout 133
Tulgren funnels 42

underwater world 88–91

voles 136

Wallace, Alfred Russell 11
Wallflower 58
wasps 78
water features 130
water fleas 127
Water Shrew 136
Water Vole 136
watercycle 123
Weasel 53
weather 104–5
whales 89, 92
whelks 94
White-clawed Crayfish 144
Whooper Swan 141
Wild Boar 54, 116

Wild Goat 117
Wild Raspberry 118
Wild Strawberry 118
Wildcat 117
winkles 94
Wood Mouse 53, 55
Wood Mushroom 62
Wren 30

Zander 132